THE POWER OF EMOTIONAL INTELLIGENCE

A CONVERSATIONAL GUIDE TO CREATE HEALTHY RELATIONSHIP HABITS, REDUCE STRESS & SUCCEED IN YOUR CAREER

CHARLES HEARN

TABLE OF CONTENTS

INTRODUCTION

Have you ever heard the story of Phineas Gage? In 1848, this railroad foreman suffered a horrifying accident when a metal rod pierced his skull, destroying much of his frontal lobe (Ratiu et al., 2004). Miraculously, Gage survived, but his personality was irrevocably altered. The once capable and even-tempered man became impulsive, volatile, socially inappropriate, and prone to angry outbursts. He could no longer read social cues, struggled to follow plans, and his formerly reliable decision-making became reckless. His drastic transformation offered a chilling early example of how damage to the brain's emotional centers can profoundly impact our behavior, relationships, and our very sense of self.

Sadly, a lack of emotional intelligence (EI) can be just as destructive. Even brilliant individuals can unknowingly sabotage their careers and relationships due to unmanaged emotions and poor communication. Without EI, raw intellect and talent often aren't enough to ensure success or happiness.

So why, then, does developing EI often feel like an afterthought? We prioritize standardized test scores, but neglect to teach children how to understand their feelings and build empathy. We chase promotions, but overlook the importance of strong, supportive teams. This stems partially from a long history of prioritizing "hard" skills in education and the workplace, a legacy of early psychological theories like behaviorism, which focused purely on observable actions rather than internal experiences. Emotions themselves were often seen as signs of weakness rather than valuable signals to be managed.

This attitude permeates much of modern culture, where the "grind" mentality is praised. Expressing genuine emotions, whether sadness, frustration, or even vulnerability can be mislabeled as "unprofessional," discouraging honest communication that's vital for building trust. Worse yet, toxic positivity, with its relentless focus on forced optimism, discourages the healthy processing of difficult feelings. This creates an emotional pressure cooker, making it harder to develop the self-awareness and emotional regulation skills essential for true EI.

Consequently, most schools still lack dedicated EI curriculums. Instead of a holistic approach to education, the primary focus remains on those standardized tests and measurable skills in core subjects. This leaves little room for teaching students about their own emotions, effective conflict resolution, or the skills needed to build healthy relationships, despite the profound impact these elements have on overall well-being and long-term success. Many teachers themselves lack formal training in EI, making it difficult for them to effectively model these skills or create a classroom environment that supports students' emotional growth. Compounding the issue is the lingering stigma around mental health struggles. Even when students need support, limited resources and social pressures can create an environment where seeking help for emotional challenges feels less valid than seeking help for academic ones.

Many workplaces also perpetuate a culture that values immediate results and overwork, leaving little room for the time and effort needed to cultivate deep relationships and individual emotional growth. This manifests through a narrow focus on short-term metrics, where behaviors like building rapport with colleagues or offering mentorship lack an immediate, quantifiable benefit. Overloaded and chronically stressed employees struggle to manage their own emotions effectively, inhibiting their ability to practice active listening or be fully present in interactions. The pressure to always appear capable discourages the vulnerability and openness needed to build trust. With the focus solely on output, team dynamics are often neglected, hindering opportunities for the type of collaboration and conflict resolution that can foster emotional growth.

While awareness of EI's importance is growing, changing ingrained systems is a slow process. This leaves it up to individuals like you to recognize the transformative power of EI and take charge of your own development, even when the world at large hasn't quite caught up. This book is your guide to doing exactly that. The RISE framework offers a roadmap for transforming your life:

- **Recognition (R):** Uncover the foundational truths of emotional intelligence, why it matters, and how it impacts every aspect of your life. Explore the core principles of EI and the role it plays in personal fulfillment and overall success.
- **Integration Strategies (IS):** Learn practical tools to master your emotions, navigate challenging situations with confidence, and build stronger, more meaningful relationships at work, at home, and with yourself. This includes strategies for stress management, building healthy

communication patterns, and applying EI principles throughout your daily life.

- **Empowerment (E):** Discover the keys to continuous EI growth, cultivating a supportive environment that propels you forward on your journey. Learn how to overcome obstacles that might derail your progress, find a community that encourages your development, and maintain your EI practice for lifelong benefits.

This book is your shortcut to the life-changing benefits of EI. Imagine the impact of deep self-awareness, understanding the way your emotions, triggers, and strengths guide your choices. This empowers you to make intentional decisions aligned with your values, creating a life that feels authentic and purposeful.

EI transforms your relationships. With empathy and trust as the foundation, you'll build stronger bonds with everyone you interact with, from loved ones to colleagues and even strangers. Conflicts become less fraught as understanding replaces defensiveness, and genuine connection becomes the norm.

While stress is an inevitable part of life, strong EI gives you unshakable resilience. Setbacks don't derail you; instead, you'll find the inner strength to adapt, bounce back, and use challenges as fuel for growth.

In your career, you'll face complex workplace dynamics with ease, communicate effectively to build influence, and earn the respect of those around you. You'll become the kind of leader who inspires others, achieving extraordinary results not through force or fear, but through genuine connection and empowerment.

Beyond these specific benefits, as your EI grows, you'll develop an unwavering sense of personal power. You'll know, deep down, that you have the inner resources to handle any challenge, creating a life defined by confidence and purpose.

Think of how Brené Brown's work has shifted our understanding of vulnerability and shame. Her groundbreaking research and relatable storytelling resonate on a deeply human level, fostering connection and empowering individuals to embrace authenticity. In her books and TED talks, she models the power of EI: owning her own imperfections, speaking from the heart, and creating space for others to do the same.

Or consider Steve Jobs' evolution from a difficult leader to a more emotionally intelligent one. While his brilliance was always there, as he developed a better understanding of his emotions and the impact they had on others, he was able to channel that brilliance more effectively, ultimately transforming Apple. Instead of demoralizing his team with outbursts, he learned to practice active listening and offer constructive feedback, building trust and inspiring greater innovation (Isaacson, 2012).

These public figures mastered the power of self-awareness, emotional management, and social skills—core components of EI that this book will teach you.

But perhaps their triumphs feel a world away from your own reality, leaving you wondering how to bridge the gap between where you are now and achieving such a remarkable transformation. Let's be honest about the day-to-day struggles that make change seem so difficult:

- **Workplace Stress:** The relentless pressure to juggle deadlines and conflicting priorities leads to burnout, damaging your mental health and impacting your ability to be present with loved ones outside of work.

- **Relationship Challenges:** Balancing work commitments with quality time for loved ones feels impossible. This breeds guilt and resentment, eroding the very connections that should be your source of support, creating a vicious cycle.
- **Self-Doubt:** When challenges arise, your inner critic takes over, questioning your capabilities and worth. This sabotages your confidence, leading to missed opportunities and a sense of stagnation.
- **Emotional Regulation:** High-pressure situations, whether at work or at home, can trigger outbursts of anger, anxiety that paralyzes you in important moments, or hurt feelings that fester into resentment. This behavior not only damages relationships but also undermines your professional reputation, making it harder to gain trust and influence within your team.
- **Communication Issues:** Finding the right words, particularly when it comes to expressing needs and giving constructive feedback, feels fraught. Misunderstandings pile up, creating distance instead of the connection you crave, both at work and in your personal life.

Imagine a different life, where conflicts dissolve through understanding, stress is met with resilience, and deep, fulfilling connections become the norm. Picture relationships defined by empathy and trust, where you feel empowered to express yourself authentically and confidently navigate life's inevitable challenges with a sense of inner strength. That's the power of emotional intelligence, and it's within your grasp. That transformation starts with the knowledge and tools within these pages. You're here because, deep down, you sense the potential that EI holds.

Are you ready to RISE?

CHAPTER ONE
BEING EMOTIONALLY INTELLIGENT

For much of the 20th century, intelligence quotient (IQ)—a measure of cognitive abilities—was seen as the most important factor in achievement. This may be because IQ is easy to measure, and higher scores often correlate with better grades and higher job performance. But, research shows that a staggering 90% of top performers have high emotional intelligence (Bradberry & Greaves, 2009). This striking statistic suggests something crucial: While IQ matters, it isn't the whole story.

Emotional intelligence (EI) is a potent ingredient in the recipe for success. It influences our relationships, our careers, and our overall well-being. Understanding and intelligently managing the powerful world of emotions—both our own and those of others— is essential for navigating the complexities of life and achieving our goals.

In this chapter, I'll introduce you to the fascinating world of EI. Together, we'll dive into the heart of emotional intelligence, exploring what it truly means to understand and manage your own emotions while skillfully navigating the feelings of others. We'll dive into its essential parts: self-awareness, self-regulation, motivation, empathy, and social skills—exploring how to harness each element for personal growth.

We'll also delve into the history of EI, tracing how our understanding shifted from focusing solely on IQ to recognizing the profound power of emotions in every aspect of our lives. We'll discover how emotional intelligence shapes relationships, fortifies leadership, strengthens resilience, and becomes a powerful tool for navigating conflict. I'll even highlight examples of individuals whose high EI has propelled them forward—not just in their careers, but in their lives overall.

UNDERSTANDING EI

EI is a fascinating ability that lets us understand, manage, and harness the power of our own emotions. It's more than just keeping your cool under pressure or being nice to people. Think of EI as your internal compass, guiding you through the ups and downs of life. With a strong EI foundation, you can build lasting relationships, become a resilient leader who inspires others, and navigate challenging situations with confidence. Imagine being able to understand what triggers your frustration, then channeling that energy into a productive conversation instead of an outburst. Or, consider the leader who truly connects with and motivates their team, fostering a sense of shared purpose. That's the power of emotional intelligence in action.

Let's explore the key components that make up this incredible skill set:

1. Self-awareness means having a clear understanding of your emotions, strengths, weaknesses, values, and drivers. It's like being a detective of your own mind, recognizing what you feel and why you feel it. Here's what it involves:

- **Recognizing your emotions:** Pay attention to what's happening inside you. Is your heart racing because you're excited, or because you're anxious? Notice not just the feeling, but its intensity. A small flutter of nerves before a presentation is normal, but a pounding heart and clammy hands might signal that you need to employ some calming techniques.
- **Understanding triggers:** Identify what sets off your emotional responses. Maybe traffic jams make you irritable, or praise from a colleague makes you happy. But why do those specific things trigger such reactions? Consider if it's about a fear of being late, or a deep-seated insecurity about your work. That deeper insight leads to more targeted self-management.

2. Self-regulation is about managing your emotions in a healthy way. It's not about suppressing what you feel but rather handling them in a constructive manner. Here's how:

- **Managing emotions:** Learn techniques to adjust your emotional state to one that's more productive in a particular situation. This might involve calming down when angry, cheering up when down, or even deliberately generating some excitement if you're feeling sluggish before a task.
- **Using emotions productively:** Beyond just feeling better, how can you strategically use your emotions? Harness positive feelings like enthusiasm to motivate yourself or a team. Channel a bit of frustration into focus when faced

with a difficult problem. Intelligently use your emotions to your advantage.

3. Motivation is about what drives you internally. We're not talking about external rewards, like money or fame. It's your personal fuel for achieving goals and finding satisfaction in what you do. It includes:

- **Internal drive:** Being passionate about your work or hobbies because they resonate with your core values. For example, a healthcare worker driven by a desire to make a difference might feel less burdened by long hours than someone purely focused on their paycheck.
- **Aiming to achieve goals:** Setting targets and enjoying the journey toward reaching them, not just the destination. This type of motivation helps you stay engaged even when things get tough.
- **Finding purpose:** Understanding how your tasks contribute to the bigger picture, giving your actions more meaning. If you're unsure of your overarching purpose, that's okay! Consider how even small goals—like finishing a project on time, or making a colleague smile—create a sense of fulfillment.

4. Empathy is the ability to put yourself in someone else's shoes and respond in an intimate and understanding way. It's essential for building strong relationships, both personally and professionally. Practicing empathy means:

- **Understanding others' perspectives:** Actively try to see things from the other person's point of view. This goes beyond just listening to their words —consider their background, experiences, and what might be influencing their emotions. A stressed-out coworker might not be rude, they might genuinely be overwhelmed.

- **Offering genuine support:** This means responding in a way that validates the other person's feelings and shows you care, even if you don't fully agree with or understand their perspective. Empathy helps you navigate disagreements without defensiveness, and can help you find common ground to work towards solutions.

5. Social skills are the tools you use to communicate and interact with others effectively. They help you build and maintain healthy relationships. This involves:

- **Effective communication:** Expressing yourself clearly, and listening actively to understand others. True communication is two-way, and your nonverbal cues (tone of voice, body language) are as important as the words you choose.
- **Teamwork:** Collaborating with others, valuing their input, and making an effort to work towards common goals even when you might disagree on the best approach. Empathy is your key to navigating diverse perspectives within teams.
- **Relationship building:** Nurturing connections with others by being a positive, supportive presence. This includes resolving conflicts constructively, building trust through consistency, and celebrating the successes of others.

These concepts might not seem interconnected at first glance, but the true power of EI becomes more obvious when you see how they come together in a real-world situation. Feeling nervous about public speaking—like delivering a presentation at work—that's something we've all felt at one time or another. Using that example, let's take a look at how the key components of EI work in action.

Imagine you've been asked to present the results of your team's latest project at a large industry conference. Despite your expertise, you can't help but feel those pre-presentation jitters, especially when you're speaking in front of a large group.

Self-awareness

- You recognize your anxiety about public speaking and acknowledge the physical symptoms, such as a racing heart and trembling hands.
- Because you know this tends to happen, you prepare extensively, anticipating questions and practicing your speech to build confidence.

Self-regulation

- To manage your anxiety, you employ some breathing techniques and positive self-talk before taking the stage.
- You set personal standards for your performance, focusing on delivering value rather than achieving perfection.
- Giving yourself that grace allows you to channel your nervousness into focused energy, infusing your presentation with a spark.

Motivation

- You're motivated by helping others—your intrinsic motivation is to share valuable insights to help others in your field.
- You also have a professional development goal of improving your public speaking skills.

- These keep you going, practicing and refining your presentation, even when it feels hard, or when you'd rather be doing something else.

Empathy

- You consider your audience, understanding that they are there to learn and gain insights.
- Although they may work in your field, the audience also consists of non-experts. You adapt your speech to keep it accessible, and avoid unnecessary jargon.

Social Skills

- You begin with an ice-breaker—a relatable anecdote to connect with your audience. As a bonus, it also reduces your own nervousness.
- During the Q&A, you listen actively to the questions, respond thoughtfully, and maintain eye contact, which encourages engagement and a two-way dialogue.

As you can see, these components work in tandem, not in isolation. The ways in which they interact to shape our experiences have fascinated thinkers for centuries. The dynamic relationship between self-awareness, self-regulation, motivation, empathy, and social skills has not only been the subject of philosophical discourse but has also been examined through the lens of history.

HISTORICAL PERSPECTIVE AND EVOLUTION OF EI CONCEPTS

While EI might feel like a modern trend, the questions at its core are timeless. Let's go back in time to explore the evolution of EI concepts, discovering how thinkers throughout history have grappled with the complex power of emotions:

- Charles Darwin (1800s): His work, *The Expression of the Emotions in Man and Animals* (Darwin, 1872), didn't just theorize about emotions—it fundamentally changed how we understand the natural world. Darwin showed how emotions are universal, serving as communication tools crucial to survival in both humans and animals. His insights laid the groundwork for modern evolutionary psychology.
- Edward Lee Thorndike (1920s and 1930s): Thorndike introduced the concept of "social intelligence," recognizing that the ability to understand and navigate social interactions is crucial for success (Thorndike & Stein, 1937). His work pushed educational practices away from rote learning and purely academic focus, advocating for the development of the whole person—including their social-emotional skills.
- Abraham Maslow (1950s): Humanistic psychologist Abraham Maslow, known for his "hierarchy of needs," believed that emotional needs are fundamental to human motivation (Maslow, 1950). His work challenged the prevailing view that focused solely on external rewards, arguing that inner fulfillment and a sense of belonging are essential for achieving our full potential.
- Howard Gardner (1970s): Howard Gardner's exploration of multiple intelligences in his book, *The Shattered Mind* (1975), revolutionized how we think about intelligence and human potential. His theory paved the way for recognizing the importance of other abilities beyond traditional IQ measures.

- Wayne Payne (1980s): In his doctoral dissertation, *A study of emotion: developing emotional intelligence; self-integration; relating to fear, pain and desire* (Payne, 1985), Payne first used the term "emotional intelligence," giving a name to this growing area of study.
- Reuven Bar-On (1980s): Bar-On created one of the first ways to measure emotional intelligence, focusing on the skills and abilities linked to our emotional wellbeing and success (Bar-On, 1988). This development helped push EI beyond theory and into practical application.
- John Mayer and Peter Salovey (1990): These psychologists provided a clear definition of EI, describing it as our ability to recognize, use, and manage our own feelings (Mayer & Salovey, 1993). Their framework made EI a skill that can be learned and strengthened, opening the door for personal and professional development.
- David Caruso (1990s): Caruso's primary focus was on human resource management and organizational behavior. His interest in emotions within the workplace was present, but not central to the formal EI discussion. It was the collaboration with Salovey and Mayer that pushed Caruso into the EI field. In the late 1990s, they developed the initial version of the Mayer-Salovey-Caruso Emotional Intelligence Test (Mayer et al., 2003). This was a critical moment in EI history, as it put forth one of the most influential ability-based models of emotional intelligence.
- Daniel Goleman (1995): Goleman made EI a household term with his best-selling book, *Emotional Intelligence* (1995). He brought the concept to the mainstream, emphasizing that our emotional skills are essential for success in all areas of life, making everyone—from leaders to parents—think more deeply about the power of feelings.

As we've seen, the concept of EI has undergone a fascinating trans-formation. From philosophical musings on the power of emotions to the development of concrete assessment tools, our under-standing of EI has grown tremendously. But it's important to remember that the way we manage our emotions has real-world consequences—and history provides stark examples.

The evolution of EI reveals more than just shifting theories. Understanding and managing our emotions—or failing to do so—has profoundly shaped the course of history. Consider Napoleon Bonaparte: a brilliant strategist, yet his volatile temper and unchecked ego fueled impulsive decisions that alienated allies and ultimately contributed to his downfall. His example illustrates a sobering truth: A lack of EI can undermine even the greatest intel-lectual potential. Napoleon's downfall serves as a stark reminder that the way we manage our emotions leaves a lasting mark on the world.

RECOGNIZING THE IMPORTANCE OF EI

Unlike the fleeting nature of feelings themselves, the consequences of our emotional responses endure. Imagine a conductor leading an orchestra. A conductor with a deep understanding of music (IQ) can create a technically sound performance. But a conductor who also understands the emotions of the musicians (EI) can inspire a truly captivating experience—one that resonates long after the final note fades. EI allows us to not just play the notes, but to infuse them with passion, adapt to the dynamics of the group, and connect with the audience on a deeper level. This applies to all aspects of life. In the workplace, EI fosters collabora-tion, innovation, and effective communication. In our personal lives, it strengthens our relationships, builds empathy, and helps us navigate challenging situations with grace and understanding. It builds our resilience and contributes to our adaptability.

We have so many examples of public figures, celebrities, and leaders who demonstrate high EI. From boardrooms to television studios, these individuals understand the importance of emotions in shaping their success. For example, Indra Nooyi, Richard Branson, Jack Welch, Satya Nadella, and Oprah Winfrey have not only revolutionized their industries but also inspired us with their emotional intelligence.

- Indra Nooyi, former CEO of PepsiCo, would write personal letters of congratulations to the parents of employees who performed exceptionally (Ward, 2017). She understood the importance of recognizing the role of family in supporting success.
- Richard Branson, founder of Virgin Group, fosters a work environment where employees feel comfortable sharing ideas, making mistakes, and taking calculated risks (Schwantes, 2023). He famously avoids punishing failure, instead viewing it as a step towards innovation.
- Jack Welch, former CEO of General Electric, would give handwritten notes to employees (Goudreau, 2013). He would do this to praise good work, but also to share constructive feedback. The fact that Welch valued direct communication and personalized feedback demonstrates strong relationship-building skills.
- When Satya Nadella, CEO of Microsoft, made an insensitive comment that caused a negative reaction, he acknowledged his error and used the opportunity to start a conversation about unconscious bias (Tublin, 2014). His self-awareness allowed him not only to willingly and

readily admit his mistake, but to turn a challenging situation into a learning opportunity.

- And finally, Oprah Winfrey, media mogul and philanthropist, was known for encouraging vulnerability and emotional openness in her guests. She was clearly able to create a safe space for others to express their emotions, allowing her to connect in a meaningful way not just with her guests, but the audience, too.

These leaders, with their diverse styles, teach us valuable lessons. Whether it's Nooyi's focus on connection, Branson's customer-centric approach, Welch's direct communication, Nadella's open-mindedness, or Oprah's skill in fostering vulnerability—they all exemplify the power of emotional intelligence. Their stories illustrate how EI transcends boardrooms and studios, positively impacting all aspects of life.

But understanding emotional intelligence is just the start. The real adventure lies in applying these principles to our own lives. How can we become more self-aware, empathetic, and adaptable? How can we harness our emotions to build stronger relationships, resolve conflicts, and navigate life's complexities? Join us in the next chapter as we explore practical ways to cultivate our emotional intelligence for personal growth and success.

CHAPTER TWO

PERSONAL DEVELOPMENT

"In a high-IQ job pool, soft skills like discipline, drive, and empathy mark those who emerge as outstanding."

— DANIEL GOLEMAN (2011)

Daniel Goleman's words cut to the heart of personal development. While we often focus on boosting our intelligence and technical skills, it's the "soft skills" of EI that truly set us apart. It bridges the gap between what you know and how effectively you apply that knowledge to achieve your goals.

BUILDING SKILLS FOR PERSONAL GROWTH

The "soft skills" of EI are truly a catalyst for personal growth. In this section, we'll start by delving into our emotions, to deepen our understanding of how they lay the groundwork for a more fulfilling and resilient life. Then, we'll explore the ways EI empowers us to build strong relationships, think clearly in challenging situations, make better decisions, and set goals that align with our deepest values. This exploration will set the stage for the next crucial step: cultivating self-awareness.

Understanding Emotions

Let's start with the "primary colors" of our emotional palette: anger, sadness, fear, disgust, surprise, and joy. These basic emotions have evolved to serve specific functions. Anger might signal a boundary violation, sadness could indicate a loss, and joy often accompanies positive experiences that benefit us.

Emotions aren't just thoughts; they have a physical dimension too. Tuning into your body can provide valuable clues. Anger might make your chest tighten, sadness might feel like a heaviness in your limbs, or, like we discussed in Chapter 1, anxiety might trigger trembling hands or a racing heart. Recognizing these physical sensations helps us understand not only what we're feeling but also the intensity of the emotion. Body awareness is a powerful tool for developing emotional intelligence.

However, emotions are rarely clear-cut. Just like colors blend into countless shades, our feelings exist on a spectrum of subtlety and complexity. That's why developing a rich emotional vocabulary helps us identify and understand these internal states with more precision. For example, when you're feeling "bad," are you actually feeling frustrated, disappointed, anxious, or perhaps overwhelmed? The more specific your understanding of the emotion, the better equipped you are to address its root cause. There's a resource, called a Feelings Wheel, that can help if you have trouble identifying more complex emotions. Today's wheels have come a long way since the original (Willcox, 1982). Calm, a subscription-based app offering guided meditations, sleep stories, and other tools to promote relaxation, focus, and sleep, has a beautiful and elaborate version of the wheel on their blog (The Feelings Wheel: Unlock the power of your emotions, 2023).

EI and Relationships

Our lives are enriched by meaningful connections with others. EI allows us to navigate the complex nature of interpersonal relationships with more skill and sensitivity. At the heart of this lies empathy—the ability to understand and share the feelings of others. EI helps us see the world through another person's eyes, leading to greater understanding and compassion. Think of a time you shared a deep connection with a friend who truly "got" what you were going through. That feeling of connection is a powerful example of EI in action.

Beyond empathy, EI transforms how we communicate. When we're aware of our own emotions, we can choose to express them in ways that don't harm others. It helps us listen actively, focus on what the other person is truly saying, and respond with respect even during disagreements. EI also plays a vital role in conflict resolution. Instead of reacting defensively or shutting down, a person with strong EI acknowledges emotions, seeks common ground, and works toward solutions that benefit everyone involved.

Finally, EI is essential for establishing healthy boundaries. When you understand and respect your own needs and limits, you can communicate them clearly to others. This allows you to build relationships where your emotional well-being is valued, fostering trust and mutual respect. Healthy boundaries are essential not only in our romantic partnerships but in our friendships, families, and even in our workplaces.

EI, Problem-Solving, and Adaptability

Life is filled with challenges, both big and small. EI has the power to transform how we approach problems and navigate difficult situations. When strong emotions like fear, frustration, or panic arise, they can cloud our thinking. It's easy to get stuck in a reactive mode or shut down completely. EI offers an antidote by helping us create a space between emotions and actions. This pause allows us to identify how our emotions are impacting our thought process and gives us a chance to manage them before making rash choices.

Think of a challenging problem, like navigating a dense forest. Strong emotions are like a thick fog—they obscure solutions and make it easy to walk in circles. EI helps that fog lift, revealing clearer paths. With self-awareness, you might realize that anxiety drives your impulse to make a hasty decision. This awareness allows you to step back, employ calming techniques, and approach the problem from a more balanced perspective. EI doesn't guarantee that there won't be hurdles, but it allows you to navigate them with more composure and clarity.

While strong negative emotions can hinder our ability to think clearly, positive emotions offer a distinct advantage in problem-solving. Feelings like joy, curiosity, and optimism can enhance our cognitive flexibility (Wang et al., 2017). This means we're better able to see connections we might miss when feeling angry or overwhelmed. Positive emotions expand our "thought-action repertoire," opening us up to new possibilities and strategies. They help us look beyond the obvious and tap into our creativity. In day-to-day life, this might look like an increased willingness to ask for input from others, consider unconventional approaches, or persist through setbacks with an upbeat attitude.

Building on that idea, EI fuels adaptability. In a constantly changing world, being able to pivot our thinking and adjust our strategies is crucial. EI helps us see that obstacles aren't impediments—they're opportunities to learn and grow. We become more open-minded, willing to explore different perspectives and find creative solutions. Instead of rigid thinking fueled by frustration, we open ourselves up to resourcefulness by having a calm, solution-focused mindset.

EI and Decision-Making

We make countless decisions every day, ranging from minor choices to major life-altering ones. EI has the potential to guide you towards decisions that align with your values and goals. Emotions like excitement, fear, or a desire for immediate gratification can cloud judgment. For example, rushing into a purchase fueled by fleeting excitement might lead to regret, whereas fear might lead you to avoid making a decision altogether, causing you to miss out on an opportunity.

Here's are a few ways that EI can empower us to navigate this complex terrain:

- Helps to recognize how *emotions influence decision-making*. For example, if you're feeling anxious about an upcoming career change, EI encourages you to explore if that fear is based on realistic concerns or if it's stemming from fear of the unknown. This awareness creates space between the emotion and the decision.
- Provides tools for *managing emotions during the decision-making process*. Emotions can feel like a powerful storm. There's no way to stop the storm, but you can learn to navigate it skillfully. Tools like mindfulness or calming

self-talk can help create mental distance from emotional turmoil, giving you the clarity needed to weigh options rationally.

Ultimately, EI leads to wiser, more informed choices. You'll learn to balance gut instincts with careful consideration, avoiding impulsive actions that might lead to regret. EI helps you connect your decisions to your deepest values, so your choices serve your long-term happiness and fulfillment.

EI, Motivation, and Goal-Setting

Achieving our dreams requires not just technical skills but also a deep source of motivation that helps us stay the course. EI plays a crucial role in fueling motivation and guiding us towards our goals:

- **It strengthens our connection to our "why."** When we understand the deep motivations behind our goals, they become more than abstract ideas. Maybe that goal of financial independence ties to your desire for freedom and flexibility. Connecting your goals back to your core values keeps you emotionally invested throughout the process.
- **It helps to manage the inevitable emotional swings that accompany any pursuit.** Setbacks, self-doubt, and frustration are a natural part of the journey. EI doesn't make these vanish, but it equips you with the tools to navigate disappointment without giving up. You'll learn to recognize when those negative emotions signal a need to adjust your approach, seek help, or simply take a break to recharge.

- **It promotes a positive, resilient mindset.** Instead of dwelling on mistakes, you learn from them with a growth-oriented attitude. When progress seems slow, EI helps you recognize and celebrate even small wins, maintaining your enthusiasm and fueling your determination to keep moving forward.

This resilient spirit is essential for staying motivated and ultimately achieving your goals.

Now that we've explored how EI empowers us to understand our emotions and how that applies to the skills of building strong relationships, solving problems effectively, making informed decisions, and staying motivated, we're ready to apply what we know. Self-awareness is like the foundation—the key to applying EI strategically to your life.

FROM UNDERSTANDING TO SELF-AWARENESS

Imagine you have all the tools you need to build yourself a beautiful house. But without a blueprint or an understanding of how to use those tools, you're limited by guesswork. Self-awareness provides that blueprint, revealing how your emotions, thought patterns, and behaviors shape your life. This knowledge allows you to apply your EI skills with precision and build the life you truly want.

But what exactly do we mean by self-awareness? It's the ability to turn your attention inward and examine how your actions, thoughts, and feelings align with your core beliefs and values. This involves understanding your emotional landscape, recognizing your strengths and areas for growth, and being mindful of how others perceive you.

The concept itself isn't new—philosophers have pondered self-knowledge for centuries. But in the modern world, the term "self-awareness" gained prominence in the 1970s thanks to psychologists Shelley Duval and Robert Wicklund (Duval & Wicklund, 1973). Their groundbreaking work focused on how we compare ourselves to our internal standards.

Today, we recognize that self-awareness is a complex, ever-evolving process. It's the key that unlocks personal growth, stronger relationships, and a deeper sense of well-being. To truly know ourselves, we must look both inward and outward. Understanding our inner world informs how we navigate the external one, and insights into how we're perceived allow us to identify areas where we can grow and become our best selves.

Internal Self-Awareness: Knowing How You Operate

- **Understanding your core self:** This includes your values, your deep motivations, and the things that truly matter to you. When you know what drives you, your choices and actions gain purpose and direction.
- **Emotional awareness:** Being able to identify and understand your emotions as they arise is key. This involves recognizing triggers, how emotions manifest in your body, and the thought patterns they often influence.
- **Identifying strengths and weaknesses:** An honest assessment of your skills, talents, and areas for growth creates a roadmap for self-improvement and allows you to leverage your strengths to compensate for weaknesses.

External Self-Awareness: Knowing How You're Experienced

- **Perception vs. intention:** There's often a gap between how we intend to come across and how we're actually perceived by others. Actively seeking feedback and observing how others react to you provides valuable data to bridge this gap.
- **Impact on others:** Self-awareness helps us recognize how our words, actions, and even our subtle nonverbal cues affect those around us. This is essential for building strong relationships and navigating social situations.
- **Areas for improvement:** Understanding how others perceive us reveals blind spots and allows us to modify our behavior for greater effectiveness in communication, collaboration, and leadership.

The Interplay: Why Both Matter for Growth

Internal and external self-awareness are like two sides of the same coin. True growth happens when you cultivate an understanding of both:

- Without internal awareness, you risk chasing external validation or goals that don't align with your values.
- Without external awareness, you might have blind spots that hinder your progress or lack the social skills needed to build strong relationships.

Now that we've explored what self-awareness is and why it matters, are you curious about your current level? The Johari Window, a classic model for assessing self-awareness, can illuminate aspects of yourself that are visible to others, those you keep hidden, and even parts of yourself waiting to be discovered.

ASSESSING SELF-AWARENESS: THE JOHARI WINDOW

The Johari Window, created by psychologists Joseph Luft and Harrington Ingham (Luft & Ingham, 1961), offers a simple but powerful framework for understanding different aspects of self-awareness. It has four quadrants:

1. Open Area (known to self, known to others): This includes your skills, behaviors, and personality traits that you and others recognize.
2. Blind Area (unknown to self, known to others): These are things others see about you that you might be unaware of, such as habits, communication quirks, or how certain emotions make you act.
3. Hidden Area (known to self, unknown to others): This encompasses your private thoughts, feelings, vulnerabilities, or motivations that you keep to yourself.
4. Unknown Area (unknown to self, unknown to others): This represents aspects of yourself yet to be discovered—hidden potential, unconscious patterns, or unexplored talents.

Here's an example of what it looks like:

	Known to Self	Unknown to Self
Known to Others	I - Open Area	II - Blind Area
Unknown to Others	III - Hidden Area	IV - Unknown Area

How to Use the Johari Window for Self-Reflection

Expanding the Open Area: Practice sharing more. Here are some questions for self-reflection:

- "What are my core values?"
- "What brings me genuine joy or fulfillment?"

Focusing on the Blind Area: Ask for honest feedback from trusted friends, colleagues, or a mentor. Here are some questions to guide them:

- "What's one strength of mine that I might not fully recognize?"
- "Is there a habit or behavior of mine that could get in my way?"
- "How do I react in stressful situations?"

Unlocking the Hidden Area: This area holds your secrets, fears, and dreams—the parts of you that remain concealed from even yourself—demanding deep introspection. Commit to practices that help to increase self-awareness:

- "What's a childhood memory that still influences my choices?"
- "If I could change one thing about myself, what would it be?"
- "What are my hidden fears or insecurities that may hold me back?"

Exploring the Unknown: Engage in self-reflection techniques. Consider journaling prompts:

- "What patterns seem to repeat in my relationships or career?"
- "What's a major life challenge I overcame, and what did I learn?"

The Johari Window is a powerful tool for self-discovery, but the journey doesn't end there. As you actively cultivate self-awareness, your blind spots shrink, and your strengths and vulnerabilities become clearer. Now, let's explore practical tips and techniques to accelerate this process and keep expanding your window of self-knowledge.

Becoming More Self-Aware: Practical Tips

The Johari Window helps us see where we stand, but true growth and self-discovery come from actively expanding our self-awareness. Here are some practical ways to nurture this crucial skill:

- **Quieting the Mind—Mindfulness and Meditation**: Our thoughts race all day long, making it hard to notice our inner world. Meditation teaches you to observe your thoughts and emotions without getting swept away by them. This creates the mental space for deep self-reflection.
- **Journaling—Mapping Your Inner Landscape**: Writing down your thoughts and experiences illuminates patterns you might not consciously recognize. Journaling prompts can guide you even deeper—consider reflecting on your emotional reactions, recurring themes in your life, or personal challenges you've faced.
- **Feedback—Expanding Your Perspective:** We all have blind spots. Actively seeking feedback from people that you trust provides valuable insights into how you are

perceived by others. Be open to their perspective, even if it's initially challenging to hear.

- **Opening Up—Seeking Support:** Meaningful conversations with friends or family can reveal aspects of yourself that are hidden even from you. Sharing your hopes, fears, and dreams allows those who know you well to reflect back parts of yourself you might be missing.
- **Objectivity—Stepping Outside of Yourself:** It's easy to get caught up in self-judgment. Try to approach your thoughts and behaviors with curiosity rather than criticism. A good strategy is to imagine you're observing a friend. This more objective stance can help you see yourself more clearly.

Be patient with yourself, celebrate your progress, and enjoy the process of self-discovery. The clearer you see your inner workings, the better equipped you'll be to manage them. This is where self-regulation comes in. While self-awareness is understanding your-self, self-regulation is about taking charge and skillfully navigating your emotions and reactions.

FROM AWARENESS TO ACTION

When I think of self-regulation, one image comes to mind: marsh-mallows.

Psychologist Walter Mischel was a pioneer in the study of self-regulation. His famous "marshmallow test" conducted back in the 1960s shed light on a crucial aspect of human behavior: the ability to delay gratification (Mischel, 2015). In his experiments, children were offered a treat (often a marshmallow) and given a choice: eat it right away, or wait and receive a larger reward. Their ability to resist temptation predicted their success and well-being later in life. Self-regulation is like those marshmallows—resisting immediate impulses in favor of long-term goals.

In short, self-regulation can be defined as the ability to control our thoughts, emotions, and behaviors to achieve our goals. It's about intentionally choosing actions that align with our long-term well-being, even when strong urges push us in other directions. While early research emphasized internal willpower, our understanding of self-regulation continues to evolve and deepen.

Beyond Willpower: Early models focused heavily on self-control as a purely internal force. We now recognize that numerous factors influence our ability to regulate ourselves, including:

- Motivation: Having a strong "why" behind your goals makes resisting temptation easier.
- Environment: Our surroundings play a significant role. It's harder to stick to a healthy diet when tempting snacks are everywhere.
- Stress Levels: When we're mentally and emotionally depleted, self-regulation suffers.
- Beliefs: Your mindset matters. Believing that willpower is a finite resource sets you up for failure. But, if you think you have the inner strength to push through, you're more likely to succeed.

The Brain and Self-Regulation: Neuroscience now sheds light on the complex interplay of brain regions involved in self-regulation. The "hot" emotional system and the rational "cool" system often compete, and understanding this dynamic helps us develop effective self-regulation strategies.

Strategies, Not Just Traits: Rather than viewing self-control as a fixed personality trait, research now emphasizes that self-regulation can be improved through deliberate practice and specific techniques, such as:

- **Mindfulness:** Noticing your emotions without judgment allows you to break the impulsive reaction cycle.
- **Reframing:** Challenging unhelpful thoughts that sabotage self-control. For example, "I'll never reach this goal" might become "This is difficult, but I can take small steps forward."
- **Planning and self-monitoring:** Recognizing your triggers and proactively developing plans to manage them enhances self-regulation.

This evolving understanding empowers us to develop more targeted and effective approaches to strengthening this essential skill. Let's examine some real-life scenarios to see how the elements of emotional intelligence we've explored interact and impact our personal growth journey.

CASE STUDY: LEADERSHIP UNDER PRESSURE

Sarah, a talented project manager, is feeling overwhelmed. There's a major deadline looming, and many of her team members have fallen behind schedule. Her usual efficiency is starting to give way to a simmering frustration that threatens to boil over. She finds herself snapping at her colleagues, and she's started to lose sleep because of her anxious thoughts about the project's potential failure.

How can Sarah apply the techniques we've talked about in this chapter to work through this common workplace issue?

Understanding Emotions: Instead of ignoring her frustration or letting it escalate, Sarah takes a moment for introspection. She identifies the root emotions: fear of not delivering on time, anxiety about letting her team down, and a touch of anger at the under-performing colleagues.

Self-Awareness: Sarah recognizes how these emotions are impacting her behavior. Her irritability is straining relationships with her team, making the situation worse. She also realizes a pattern from past projects—as stress increases, her communication becomes curt and overly critical.

Self-Regulation: Understanding her triggers and patterns is the first step. Sarah employs several techniques:

- **Calming Strategies:** She takes short breaks for deep breathing to calm her nervous system.
- **Reframing:** Instead of focusing on blame, she shifts to problem-solving: "Things aren't on track, what adjustments can I make?"
- **Proactive Communication:** Sarah schedules individual check-ins with struggling team members, focusing on solutions rather than criticism. She also transparently communicates with her superiors about the challenges, seeking their support.

What impacts can Sarah expect, now that she's taken these actions?

- **Improved Outcomes:** By tackling her own emotions head-on, Sarah prevents them from sabotaging the project. Her shift towards proactive problem-solving re-energizes the team.
- **Stronger Relationships:** Showing empathy to her colleagues builds trust, making them more likely to seek help when needed.

- **Personal Growth:** Every challenging situation is an opportunity. Sarah recognizes her stress triggers and develops a toolkit for managing them, increasing her effectiveness in future leadership roles.

Key Takeaway: This example shows how emotional intelligence isn't about suppressing emotions but about recognizing them, understanding their impact, and choosing a course of action that aligns with your goals and values.

The skills we've explored—understanding our emotions, cultivating self-awareness, and practicing self-regulation—aren't just abstract concepts. They have the power to transform the way we navigate challenges and opportunities in all aspects of our lives. This is especially true in the workplace, where strong emotional intelligence can make the difference between surviving and truly thriving. Let's delve into how EI can enhance your professional success and propel you towards a fulfilling career.

CHAPTER THREE

WORKPLACE AND CAREER

Think your job description is just about your technical skills? Think again. While those hard skills get you in the door, it's your EI that determines how far you'll go. Unacknowledged but ever-present, emotions shape the modern workplace. From navigating team dynamics to addressing client conflicts, the ability to manage your own emotions and understand those around you is key to success. And today's employees are seeking more than just a paycheck—they want understanding, support, and leadership that recognizes their humanity. 74% prioritize empathy, and 70% feel that mental well-being support is critical (Goddu, 2021). EI gives you the tools to navigate this landscape, leading to success for both yourself and your organization.

This chapter explores how EI empowers you to thrive in your workplace. You'll learn practical strategies for leveraging EI to build strong relationships, resolve conflicts, communicate effectively, navigate challenging office dynamics, and foster a positive work environment. Get ready to transform how you approach your work—and watch your career soar.

THE POWER OF EI IN PROFESSIONAL ROLES

Leadership Positions

Every day, our emotions subtly, and sometimes not so subtly, shape our work lives. Whether we're conscious of it or not, how we perceive, understand, and manage our own emotions—as well as how we interpret the emotions of others—has a profound impact on our professional success. This is where emotional intelligence comes in. Research shows that variations in EI directly influence how well we navigate challenging situations, build relationships, and ultimately achieve our goals within the workplace (Cherniss, 2010). But what makes EI especially transformative for leaders?

Self-Mastery and Influence: Leaders who understand their emotions, triggers, and reactions are better equipped to handle the inevitable pressures of their roles. This self-awareness allows them to remain calm in the face of challenges, inspiring confidence in their team. Leaders with high EI are less likely to fall prey to impulsive decisions or emotional outbursts, fostering an environment of trust and stability.

Building a Thriving Team: Empathetic leadership is crucial. When leaders genuinely connect with their team members, understanding their motivations and struggles, they unlock better performance. EI-savvy leaders are in tune with the emotional climate of their team, able to proactively address issues and create a sense of belonging that drives engagement and loyalty.

Navigating Complexity: Today's work environments are constantly evolving. Leaders with strong EI have the adaptability and resilience to handle unexpected changes, pivoting their approach without becoming overwhelmed. Their ability to understand and manage their own anxieties helps them guide their team through uncertainty with clarity and confidence.

Vision and Inspiration: Effective leaders aren't just managers; they are visionaries. EI allows them to communicate their goals in a way that resonates with their team, sparking enthusiasm and commitment. They recognize that true inspiration speaks to the heart as well as the mind.

The driving forces behind leadership success—self-mastery, building a thriving team, navigating complexity, and cultivating a compelling vision—are deeply intertwined with EI. The specific way EI manifests might differ depending on a leader's chosen style. Truly effective leaders understand that success depends on their ability to influence and understand the people they lead—a skillset fundamentally rooted in EI.

Here are a few examples of common leadership styles, and the role of EI in each (Miranda, 2023):

Transformational Leadership: Focuses on inspiring and motivating team members to envision a greater future and work towards shared goals. Charisma, vision, and individualized consideration are key. Leaders with high EI excel in this style, as they are able to connect emotionally with their team and inspire them towards meaningful goals.

Transactional Leadership: Centers on the exchange of rewards and consequences to achieve results. Clear goals, expectations, and rewards for performance are emphasized. While less focused on emotional connection, EI still plays a role for transactional leaders in setting fair expectations, handling conflicts, and managing their own stress levels.

Servant Leadership: Prioritizes serving the needs of team members, fostering their growth and development. Leaders act as stewards rather than traditional authority figures. EI is at the core of servant leadership, as it requires empathy, self-awareness, and the ability to build genuine relationships based on trust.

Democratic Leadership: Emphasizes participation and collaboration in decision-making. Leaders facilitate discussion and value the team's input. EI-savvy democratic leaders actively listen, value diverse perspectives, and foster a sense of ownership that boosts team morale.

Situational Leadership: Emphasizes flexibility and adapting leadership style to fit the needs of the situation and the maturity level of team members. Leaders with strong EI are better able to assess situations, read the emotional needs of their team, and adjust their approach for optimal results.

Authentic Leadership: Focuses on leaders being true to their values and beliefs, building trust and fostering genuine connections with their team. Authenticity requires a high level of self-awareness, and EI enables leaders to navigate challenging situations in alignment with their values, inspiring trust in their team.

These are just a few examples of common leadership styles—the possibilities are far more nuanced. The most effective leaders don't rigidly adhere to a single model but demonstrate the flexibility to adapt their approach in response to different situations and the needs of their teams. This ability to assess, understand, and calibrate their leadership style is a hallmark of high EI.

Non-Leadership Positions

EI isn't just for those at the top. While the spotlight often shines on EI in leadership, its importance extends to everyone, regardless of your title. Think of it like this: While your hard skills help you do your job, your EI helps you do it well while navigating the intricacies of the workplace. From building strong relationships with colleagues to handling difficult clients with finesse, a high EI offers you distinct advantages that can propel your career forward. Here's how:

Improved Decision-Making: Self-regulation skills help employees avoid impulsive choices driven by fleeting emotions, leading to more rational and effective decisions.

Enhanced Collaboration: The ability to understand and empathize with colleagues fosters strong teamwork, making it easier to navigate disagreements constructively and create a sense of belonging.

Effective Conflict Resolution: EI allows team members to recognize the emotional undercurrents at play in conflicts, leading to successful de-escalation or the ability to find common ground.

Skillful Relationship Management: Individuals with high EI adeptly navigate complex office dynamics, building positive relationships that contribute to overall team success.

Increased Resilience: The ability to manage stress and bounce back from setbacks is crucial for thriving in any workplace. EI provides the tools for navigating challenges with a calm, focused mindset.

By developing your EI, you gain a powerful tool to excel in your current role and set the stage for future career growth. Whether it's resolving conflicts with colleagues, handling difficult clients, or proactively contributing to a positive team dynamic, EI empowers you to make a meaningful impact within your organization. And in today's workplace, where collaboration is key, those skills are more valuable than ever.

EI and Effective Collaboration

Effective collaboration hinges upon respect, trust, and open communication. EI is the vital ingredient that makes this possible. Let's break down why EI is so crucial for successful teamwork.

The Foundation of Trust: When team members understand their own emotions and are empathetic towards their colleagues, it creates a foundation of psychological safety, or feeling safe enough to take risks within a team or group, without facing negative consequences like embarrassment, rejection, or punishment. People feel comfortable sharing their ideas without the fear of judgment or ridicule, knowing their contributions will be valued.

Handling Differences with Grace: Teams are made of diverse individuals with unique perspectives. EI helps navigate inevitable disagreements with understanding and a focus on solutions. Instead of defensiveness or personal attacks, emotionally intelligent team members actively listen and address the root causes of conflict.

A Culture of Creativity: Innovation thrives in an environment where people feel comfortable taking calculated risks. EI fosters this sense of freedom, as emotionally supportive teams are less likely to shut down unconventional ideas, leading to breakthrough thinking.

Commitment and Shared Goals: EI allows team members to connect emotionally to the shared purpose. This translates into higher motivation, a willingness to go above and beyond to support team goals, and a greater resilience when facing setbacks.

Enhanced Communication: Clear, empathetic communication fuels strong and collaborative teams. EI empowers clear communication even in challenging situations, preventing misunderstandings and ensuring everyone feels valued and understood.

Teams built on EI become greater than the sum of their parts. Leaders and members with strong EI are key drivers of this transformation. When team members feel understood, valued, and supported, it translates into high levels of engagement, resulting in a collaborative work atmosphere where everyone can thrive.

EI'S IMPACT ON TEAM DYNAMICS AND WORKPLACE CULTURE

The positive effects of EI extend far beyond individual success. When employees are equipped to understand their own emotions, empathize with colleagues, and manage their responses skillfully, this creates a foundation for a more respectful, inclusive, and cooperative workplace culture. Practical actions like these can transform a good workplace into a truly inclusive one.

Creating a positive, inclusive workplace culture

The positive ripple effects of EI extend far beyond team dynamics and individual success. An EI-rich workplace cultivates a broader culture where respect, empathy, and the ability to understand diverse perspectives become the norm. This sets the stage for the practical initiatives that transform a good workplace into a truly inclusive one. These actions include:

Data-Driven Approach: Don't rely on assumptions. Utilize surveys, focus groups, and analysis of existing data to identify areas where inclusion efforts can be strengthened. Track metrics over time to measure progress.

Accessibility: Conduct regular audits of physical spaces and digital platforms to ensure accessibility for individuals with disabilities.

Inclusive Language: Words matter. Be mindful of the language used in everyday communication, policies, and company materials. Avoid generalizations, stereotypes, or language that marginalizes any group.

Supplier Diversity: Look beyond hiring practices to examine the supply chain. Seek partnerships with businesses owned by individuals from diverse backgrounds.

Safe Spaces: Create designated physical or virtual spaces where employees from diverse backgrounds feel comfortable connecting, sharing experiences, and seeking support.

Feedback Culture: Actively solicit feedback from employees at all levels. This demonstrates a genuine commitment to hearing all voices and creates a sense of ownership in shaping the workplace culture.

Expanded Holiday Calendar: Acknowledging diverse holidays fosters a sense of belonging and demonstrates respect for different cultural and religious traditions.

Mandatory Diversity Training: Training shouldn't be optional. Ensure all employees receive education on unconscious bias, inclusive communication, and strategies for creating a welcoming environment.

Diversity Training Group: Establish a dedicated group to address diversity, equity, and inclusion on an ongoing basis. This maintains focus and ensures continuous improvement.

Non-Discrimination Policy: A strong, well-communicated policy is essential. It sets a clear standard and provides a framework for addressing any concerns.

Employee Resource Groups (ERGs): ERGs provide spaces for employees with shared identities to network, advocate for their needs, and contribute to company-wide inclusion efforts.

Cross-Cultural Mentorship: Pair employees from different backgrounds to foster understanding, break down silos, and expand perspectives.

Sponsorship Programs: Sponsorship takes mentorship a step further. Set up formal programs where leaders actively advocate for talented employees from underrepresented groups, opening doors to advancement opportunities.

Representation in Leadership: Actively work to diversify leadership positions at all levels. This sends a powerful message about inclusivity and provides role models for employees from underrepresented groups.

Creating an inclusive culture is an ongoing process, not a checklist. True inclusivity requires continuous effort, reflection, and a willingness to adapt as the needs of the workforce evolve. Just as organizations must prioritize adaptability for success, the individuals within those organizations benefit greatly from developing the same mindset.

Here are practical ways you can strengthen your EI and positively impact your workplace:

Developing Empathy: The cornerstone of EI is understanding others.

- **Pay Attention:** Go beyond words. Notice body language, tone of voice, and the unspoken emotions behind interactions.
- **Active Listening:** Focus on truly hearing the other person, not just formulating your response. Ask clarifying questions to show engagement.
- **Walk in Their Shoes:** Put aside your own perspective and try to see the situation through the eyes of the other person. What concerns or pressures might be influencing their behavior?

Emotional Reasoning: Harness your own emotions for better decision-making.

- **Pause Before Reacting:** Impulsive reactions fueled by anger or frustration rarely create good outcomes. Take a moment to analyze your own emotions before responding.
- **Consider the Impact:** How will your words or actions likely make others feel? Will your choices bring you closer to your goals or create unnecessary conflict?
- **Learn From the Past:** Reflect on past situations where your emotions clouded your judgment. What could you have done differently?

Managing Your Responses: You can't control others' emotions, but you can control your own.

- **Mindfulness:** Recognize the physical signs of escalating emotions (rapid heartbeat, tension). Employ calming techniques like deep breathing to maintain composure.
- **Recognize Manipulation:** Are others using guilt or aggression to influence you? Understanding these tactics strengthens your resolve.

- **Setting Boundaries:** If a situation becomes toxic, know when to disengage respectfully. You have the right to protect your own emotional well-being.

Developing EI takes practice and patience. Start small by focusing on one aspect at a time. Regularly assess your progress and celebrate small victories. The same dedication to growth that strengthens your EI fosters the skills and confidence needed to chart your career path. As you hone your ability to understand yourself and others, navigate complex situations, and communicate effectively, you naturally empower yourself to take charge of your professional journey.

ENHANCING EI IN PROFESSIONAL ENVIRONMENTS

EI goes far beyond workplace dynamics. It empowers you to reach your full career potential and stand out in any field. Let's break down how EI translates into tangible career success:

- **Self-Awareness:** Understanding your strengths, weaknesses, values, and passions forms the foundation of a fulfilling career. EI allows you to pinpoint what truly motivates you, leading to more focused job searches and informed career decisions.
- **Staying Motivated:** The path to success is rarely without setbacks. EI provides the resilience to bounce back from disappointments, reframe challenges as opportunities, and maintain a determined focus on your long-term vision.
- **Embracing Change:** Today's careers are rarely linear. EI allows you to adapt to evolving job markets and new opportunities. Instead of fearing change, emotionally intelligent individuals approach it with flexibility, seeing it as a chance for growth.

- **Productivity and Goal Setting:** EI gives you the tools to manage distractions, stay organized, and break down ambitious goals into achievable steps. This boosts your productivity and increases your chances of success.
- **Building Strong Relationships:** EI helps cultivate strong connections with colleagues and managers, fostering a supportive environment. This support network can provide guidance, open doors, and champion your achievements.

We've seen how EI unlocks potential and distinguishes high achievers. If you're ready to see this transformation in your own career, the following actionable steps will take you from simply getting by to truly thriving:

- **Defining Your Path:** Take the time for self-reflection. What type of role excites you? What industries align with your skills and interests? Be specific—a clear goal makes planning easier.
- **SMART Goals:** Set goals that are Specific, Measurable, Achievable, Relevant, and Time-Bound. This provides clarity, breaks down larger goals, and allows you to track progress.
- **Learning Never Stops:** Dedicate yourself to continuous learning. New skills enhance your value to employers and help you adapt to changes in your field.
- **Embrace Proactivity:** Don't wait for opportunities to find you. Seek out training, volunteer for projects that stretch your skills, or find ways to add value beyond your current role.
- **Track Your Progress:** Regularly assess your progress against your goals. This allows you to make adjustments, stay motivated, and celebrate your wins.

- **Find a Mentor:** Seek out a mentor who can offer guidance, insights, and support along your career journey. A strong mentor can be an invaluable asset.
- **Join and Grow Your Network:** Proactively build relationships within your industry. Attend conferences, join relevant online communities, and connect with those you admire.

While these strategies undoubtedly boost your career prospects, there's one that stands out above the rest: a strong professional network. A well-cultivated network paves the way to hidden job opportunities, invaluable insights, and the kind of support that accelerates your growth.

Networking might initially seem intimidating, but its benefits are undeniable. Beyond the impressive fact that, according to a 2020 Jobvite study, 31% of job seekers find success through connections, a robust network grants access to insider knowledge, mentorship, and recommendations (Jobvite, 2020). These advantages put you ahead of the competition, facilitate career pivots, deepen your industry insights, and create a supportive professional community that fuels your success.

Here are some actionable ways to start building those essential connections:

Leveraging Your Existing Connections

- **Tap into your existing circle:** Start with family, friends, and former classmates. They might know people in your target field who would be happy to connect.
- **Reconnect with former coworkers:** Reach out to past colleagues—they might have helpful leads or insights.

- **Leverage your alumni association:** Many colleges and universities have strong alumni networks, offering events and resources to connect with others in your field.

Expanding Your Reach

- **Attend networking events:** Industry conferences, meetups, and workshops are excellent places to connect with like-minded professionals.
- **Get social:** LinkedIn is vital for networking. Optimize your profile and engage with others thoughtfully in relevant groups.
- **Join professional organizations:** These often offer networking events, mentorship programs, and industry-specific resources.
- **Volunteer:** Giving back is a fantastic way to build relationships with people who share your values.

Proactive Networking

- **Informational interviews:** Proactively reach out to people in roles or companies you admire and ask if they'd be willing to have a short informational chat. This allows you to learn from their experiences and build a relationship.
- **Think beyond your bubble:** Connect with people in adjacent industries—diverse perspectives can lead to unexpected opportunities.

Nurturing Connections

- **Follow Up Persistently:** After meeting someone new, don't let the connection fizzle out. Follow up with a personalized message, perhaps referencing something from your conversation or sharing a relevant article.

- **Offer Value First:** Don't approach networking as purely transactional. Think about ways you can genuinely help others—sharing resources, making introductions, or offering your skills on a small project.

Building a strong network takes time and effort. By consistently implementing these strategies, you'll gain access to a wealth of support, resources, and hidden opportunities that will accelerate your career success.

CASE STUDY: NAVIGATING A CAREER PIVOT WITH EI

Mark, an experienced marketing professional, feels unfulfilled in his current role. He yearns for work that aligns with his passions for creativity and innovation, yet lacks the clarity and direction to make the leap.

How can Mark leverage EI to navigate this career pivot?

Understanding Emotions: Mark experiences a mix of discontentment and a sense of being stuck. Instead of letting these feelings fester, he seeks support from an EI-focused coach.

Self-Awareness: Coaching helps Mark unpack his motivations, identifying core values that were misaligned with his current position. He gains clarity on his ideal work environment and the kind of projects that excite him.

Self-Regulation: Instead of fixating on the negative, Mark adopts a proactive mindset. He channels his energy towards developing strategies to find his dream role.

Proactive Communication: Equipped with increased self-aware-ness, Mark initiates honest conversations within his network. He clearly articulates his passions and goals, which leads to a surprising revelation: a hidden opportunity within his existing company.

What impacts can Mark expect, now that he's taken these actions?

- **Career Fulfillment:** By applying EI strategies, Mark successfully pivoted into a role that aligns with his passions and values. He experiences greater job satisfaction and a sense of purpose.
- **Increased Motivation:** Mark's renewed sense of engagement and the opportunity to work on innovation-focused projects revitalize his motivation and performance.
- **Personal Growth:** This successful career transition strengthens Mark's self-awareness and communication skills, fueling his continued professional growth and resilience.

Key Takeaway: This case study demonstrates the power of EI in career decisions. By understanding his emotions, communicating effectively, and proactively seeking solutions, Mark successfully navigated a career change that led to increased fulfillment and success.

CASE STUDY: MANAGING DIFFICULT EMOTIONS AND BUILDING INFLUENCE

Eve, a dedicated team leader, faces a challenging situation when she has to let go of a beloved, yet under-performing team member.

This decision weighs heavily on her, causing internal turmoil and impacting her usual confident leadership style.

How can Eve apply EI to navigate this challenging situation?

Understanding Emotions: Instead of ignoring her complex feelings, Eve takes time for honest introspection. She identifies the root emotions: guilt, self-doubt, and concern for her team's well-being.

Self-Awareness: Eve recognizes how these emotions might derail her effectiveness. She also understands the importance of clear communication and empathy during periods of change.

Self-Regulation: Eve reaches out to a mentor for guidance and support, providing a safe space to unpack her emotions and gain perspective. Additionally, she incorporates journaling and meditation to cultivate self-awareness and recenter herself emotionally.

Empathetic Communication: Equipped with this greater understanding, Eve communicates the difficult decision with compassion and conviction. She openly acknowledges the situation with her team, invites feedback, and remains focused on rebuilding trust.

What impacts can Eve expect, now that she's taken these actions?

- **Improved Outcomes:** Eve's EI prevents her emotions from hindering a difficult but necessary decision. Her proactive approach fosters a smoother transition for her team.
- **Stronger Relationships:** By combining empathy with honest communication, Eve builds trust and respect, ensuring solid team dynamics moving forward.

- **Personal Growth:** This situation provides Eve with a greater understanding of her emotional triggers and the opportunity to hone her introspection and communication skills.

Key Takeaway: This case study illustrates how combining mentorship and introspection cultivates EI. By understanding and regulating her emotions, Eve is able to navigate a difficult situation with empathy and leadership, ultimately strengthening both her team and her own leadership capabilities.

As we've seen, EI is a powerful asset in the professional landscape. It empowers you to navigate challenges, build strong relationships, and make well-informed decisions. By developing your EI, you'll unlock your full potential and position yourself for long-term success.

In the next chapter, we'll delve deeper into the transformative role of EI in fostering strong, healthy relationships. We'll explore how EI fosters empathy, communication, and conflict resolution, all essential ingredients for building a fulfilling and supportive network, both at work and in your personal life.

CHAPTER FOUR

BUILDING HEALTHY RELATIONSHIPS

T he power of connection fuels our lives. From the person we collaborate with on a project to the loved ones we share our heart with, our relationships shape our experiences. Yet those same connections can sometimes be a source of stress or frustration. The key to navigating these complexities lies in EI. Research shows that couples with stronger EI skills experience greater positivity and less conflict in their relationships (Kaur & Junnarkar, 2017).

This chapter explores how EI provides the tools to build meaningful, supportive relationships—at work, at home, and within ourselves. We'll delve into strategies that elevate your communication, deepen your empathy, and help you resolve conflicts with skill. Get ready to discover how EI can transform your relationships, allowing them to become a source of joy, support, and growth.

THE ROLE OF EI IN RELATIONSHIPS

EI isn't just a "nice to have" in relationships—it's the crucial foundation upon which strong, fulfilling connections are built. EI empowers us to understand our own emotions, perceive and empathize with the feelings of others, and communicate effectively even in challenging situations. These skills are essential for creating trust, fostering open dialogue, and navigating the inevitable ups and downs that all relationships experience.

Our emotions hold a wealth of information. At times they can feel overwhelming, but EI teaches us to view our own feelings as valuable guides. Someone skilled in EI recognizes that irritation stemming from a partner's behavior might signal an unmet need. Instead of lashing out, they can calmly express that need, initiating a constructive conversation. Likewise, EI allows us to perceive emotional cues from others. Noticing that a colleague seems withdrawn isn't just an observation—it's an opportunity to offer support or adjust our approach for more effective collaboration.

Empathy gives us the power to step outside ourselves and genuinely understand another person's perspective. In relationships, this translates to feeling heard, valued, and secure. When conflicts arise, empathy prevents defensiveness and blame, opening the door to finding solutions that honor everyone's needs. It allows us to celebrate our loved ones' successes as our own and offer meaningful support during difficult times.

As you can see, EI has a profound impact on our relationships. Let's explore the specific ways it benefits us, both in our personal and professional lives:

Understanding Ourselves and Others

- **Enhanced Understanding:** People with high EI have a deeper understanding of their own behavior and the way it influences others. In our personal lives, this translates into building stronger bonds with our loved ones, as we understand our motivations and reactions better. At work, this level of self-awareness allows us to identify potential triggers and manage our emotions in challenging situations, preventing them from sabotaging key relationships.
- **Awareness of Others' Emotions:** People with high EI are attuned to the emotional needs of those around them. This could mean truly listening and understanding a friend's struggles, leading to a deeper sense of connection, or picking up on subtle cues of frustration or disengagement from a client or team member. Proactively addressing these underlying emotions often leads to greater overall success and smoother collaborations.

Communication and Collaboration

- **Understanding Nonverbal Cues:** A significant portion of communication is nonverbal. EI helps us decode and understand the subtle signals that others send. Imagine being able to sense a romantic partner's unspoken need for reassurance or a colleague's unspoken hesitation to express a differing opinion during a project meeting. This awareness allows for greater connection and more productive conversations.
- **Improved Efficiencies:** EI-driven communication enhances clarity and cuts down on misunderstandings, boosting productivity both personally and professionally.

This might mean finally having that constructive conversation with a friend about a longstanding issue, leading to greater closeness. In a work setting, it translates into efficient meetings, clear project instructions, and reduced frustration for all involved.

Greater Emotional Regulation

Instead of being at the mercy of our emotions, EI teaches us to identify our feelings and manage them constructively. This allows healthier interactions and reduced conflict with those we care about. In the workplace, it allows us to remain calm in the face of setbacks or difficult clients, preventing emotional outbursts that could harm our professional reputation.

Positive Influence

Emotionally intelligent individuals don't just excel personally; they elevate those around them. By fostering a culture of empathy, open communication, and collaboration, they create a more positive and productive environment for everyone. This kind of influence doesn't remain within office walls. The lessons we learn about ourselves and others through EI translate into our personal lives, making us better partners, friends, and family members.

Career Advancement

People with high EI possess the interpersonal skills, emotional regulation, and ability to inspire others in ways that make them invaluable assets in the workplace. This often translates into tangible career advancement, with opportunities for leadership roles and increased professional success (Sivanjali, 2021). As we discussed in Chapter 3, the ability to build strong professional networks, navigate workplace dynamics, and manage one's own emotions are all crucial factors in achieving career goals. EI serves as the foundation upon which these skills are built, starting at those base relationships.

The benefits of EI we've explored extend far beyond personal fulfillment and career success. As social beings, our relationships are fundamental to our happiness and well-being. Those with high emotional intelligence possess a distinct set of traits that enable them to build deeply connected, healthy, and resilient relationships in all areas of their lives. These very qualities—the hallmarks of strong bonds—are what we'll explore next in individuals with high EI.

THE TRAITS OF HIGH EI IN RELATIONSHIPS

While we've addressed the core components of emotional intelligence earlier, let's now explore how self-awareness, self-regulation, motivation, empathy, and social skills are particularly crucial for fostering strong relationships. These skills form the bedrock of strong, meaningful connections, allowing us to navigate our own emotions and those of others, communicate with clarity and compassion, and build a foundation of respect, trust and understanding.

Beyond the essentials, there are additional traits that those with high EI often possess. These qualities further enrich relationships, adding depth, intimacy, and long-term sustainability:

- **Curiosity:** Actively exploring your partner's thoughts, experiences, and dreams to deepen your connection.
- **Openness:** Embracing vulnerability by sharing your authentic self and being receptive to feedback. This fosters trust and intimacy.

- **Healthy Boundaries:** Clearly communicating your needs while respecting those of your partner. This promotes a sense of both personal and relational well-being.
- **Optimism:** Maintaining a positive outlook and belief in your ability to overcome challenges together. This strengthens your bond during difficult times.
- **Playfulness:** Injecting lightheartedness and humor into your interactions. This reduces stress and keeps your connection joyful.
- **Resilience:** Bouncing back from misunderstandings or conflict by acknowledging mistakes, offering sincere apologies, and focusing on solutions.
- **Self-Sufficiency:** Maintaining interests and a support system outside the relationship, promoting independence and preventing unhealthy dependency.
- **Flexibility:** Adapting your approach or expectations based on the situation or the other person's needs. This demonstrates respect and a willingness to find common ground.
- **Trustworthiness:** Exhibiting reliability, honesty, and follow-through on commitments. This builds a foundation of security within your relationship.

While we often associate strong bonds with romantic partnerships, it's important to remember that high EI fosters healthy, lasting relationships of all kinds. Whether with friends, family members, or colleagues, the ability to understand our own needs, empathize with others, and communicate effectively is the cornerstone of positive and fulfilling connections in every sphere of our lives.

ENHANCING COMMUNICATION WITH EI

Good communication is an important part of all relationships, and an essential element of any healthy partnership. All relationships experience ups and downs, but a healthy communication style makes it easier to deal with conflict, ultimately fostering a stronger and healthier bond. Communication truly lies at the heart of how we connect with those around us.

Communicating effectively isn't always easy. Our emotions, past experiences, and differing communication styles can create road-blocks, leading to misunderstandings, hurt feelings, and damaged trust. This is where EI comes in, providing the tools to overcome these challenges and transform how we communicate within our relationships.

Clarity Through Conscious Communication

Words hold immense power in shaping relationships. EI gives us greater control over that power, allowing us to choose our words with care and awareness of their impact. Let's consider ways to use verbal communication with more consciousness:

- **Think before speaking:** Self-awareness allows us to pause and examine our words before voicing them. This reduces impulsive or hurtful comments. Example: Instead of lashing out during an argument with your partner, taking a moment to understand your anger might lead to a calmer, "I'm starting to feel overwhelmed, and I need a short break."
- **Use concise language:** Clarity and respect for your listener's time go hand in hand. EI helps us convey our

message with just the right amount of detail, avoiding long-winded explanations that risk misunderstandings.

- **Understand your audience:** Empathy allows us to tailor our communication style to the person we're speaking with. Consider their needs and perspective. For example, the way you explain a complex issue to a loved one might be very different from how you'd present it to a colleague.
- **Be mindful of your tone:** Our tone reveals as much as our words. Self-regulation helps us express ourselves while managing frustration or disappointment. This prevents escalation and maintains an openness for constructive dialogue.
- **Speak with confidence:** This isn't about being forceful. It's about self-awareness and recognizing that your voice has value. When you've reflected on your thoughts beforehand, hesitation fades, and you communicate with a natural clarity that inspires trust.
- **Show your authentic self:** Pretense undermines relationships. EI helps us shed the need to impress or appease others. This allows our true selves to emerge and fosters genuine connection. Of course, authenticity must be balanced with empathy and respect for the listener.
- **Gain feedback:** Those we trust can provide valuable insights into potential blind spots in our communication. An emotionally intelligent person is receptive to feedback, using it for growth and stronger relationships.

Understanding the Unspoken

So much of our communication happens without a single word being uttered. EI allows us to decipher these unspoken messages and adjust our own body language for greater clarity in our relationships. Let's explore this non-verbal realm:

- **Pay attention to nonverbal signals:** Observe facial expressions, posture, and gestures. EI-driven empathy lets us pick up on subtle cues of discomfort that a friend might be hesitant to express verbally, or sense a partner's excitement they may not yet have put into words.
- **Look for incongruent behaviors:** When words and body language contradict each other, it often signals a deeper issue. An emotionally intelligent person notices an incongruity like a friend saying they're fine while looking downcast. This awareness allows for a gentle, supportive inquiry rather than dismissing the mismatch.
- **Focus on tone of voice:** It's not just about the words! Sarcasm, irritation, or tenderness all come through clearly in tone. Self-regulation helps us be attuned to our own tone, ensuring we aren't sending mixed messages to those we care about.
- **Use good eye contact:** Eye contact signals attentiveness and genuine interest. EI helps us overcome shyness or the tendency to be distracted during important conversations, allowing for a deeper exchange.
- **Use signals to add meaning:** A warm smile or a reassuring touch can convey emotions deeper than words alone. Emotional intelligence allows us to use non-verbal cues with intention, fostering an unspoken sense of support and connection with loved ones.
- **Look at signals as a whole:** Avoid fixating on isolated gestures. Instead, use EI's emphasis on gaining a comprehensive understanding of the situation. Consider all their non-verbal cues in combination to glean a clearer picture of a person's emotional state.
- **Consider the context:** A furrowed brow might signal deep concentration on a task rather than annoyance. EI helps us consider the context, including the person we know, to

interpret body language correctly. This prevents the kind of misunderstandings that damage relationships.

- **Be aware that signals can be misread:** Even with the best intentions, misinterpretations can happen. EI fosters a sense of humility. This allows for a non-judgmental approach and openness to a conversation about what the non-verbal cues might truly mean.

The Power of Presence

True connection requires more than just hearing the words someone speaks. EI cultivates the art of active listening, a skill that conveys respect, builds trust, and deepens our relationships. Let's examine the elements of this powerful practice:

- **Face the speaker and have eye contact:** This simple act demonstrates focus and genuine interest. While respecting cultural differences in norms, EI helps us avoid distractions and give our full presence to the person speaking—a valuable gift in itself.
- **Don't interrupt:** Letting someone talk without interruption communicates that they and their experience are valued. Self-regulation helps us overcome the impulse to jump in with our own thoughts, even when eager to help or express a differing viewpoint.
- **Listen without judging or jumping to conclusions:** EI teaches us to set aside our own biases and assumptions, creating a space where another person can feel truly heard and understood. This non-judgmental stance promotes honesty and vulnerability in conversations.
- **Don't start planning what to say next:** It's tempting to mentally rehearse our response while someone else is speaking. However, this diminishes our ability to actively

listen. EI encourages us to stay present in the moment, trusting that we can formulate a thoughtful response later.

- **Show that you're listening:** Small cues like nodding, or neutral phrases like "I hear you" demonstrate engagement. Overdoing it risks seeming disingenuous, highlighting the importance of authenticity fueled by genuine empathy.
- **Don't impose your opinions or solutions:** Unsolicited advice can shut down a conversation. It sends the message that you see yourself as an expert rather than an empathetic listener. Self-awareness helps us recognize this tendency, fostering a humble approach that allows the other person to feel heard, not fixed.
- **Stay focused:** Our attention naturally wanders, especially in challenging or emotional conversations. EI provides us with the focus to gently guide our mind back to the present moment and the speaker's words.
- **Ask questions:** When appropriate, open-ended questions can deepen understanding and demonstrate your commitment to hearing the other person fully. However, EI guides us to avoid questions that derail the conversation or serve our own curiosity over the speaker's needs.
- **Paraphrase and summarize:** Reflecting back what you heard not only clarifies understanding, but it also shows respect and attentiveness. Example: "It sounds like you're feeling overwhelmed with the demands on your time, and you're unsure how to prioritize. Is that right?"

The art of active listening lies at the heart of strong relationships. By cultivating the attentiveness, non-judgment, and sincere engagement that EI empowers us with, we create space for genuine connection. It might seem simple, but offering someone the gift of your full presence is transformative. This focus on truly hearing another person sets the stage for the deeper skill of empathy—the ability to step into their shoes and understand their world.

Empathy in Action

The skills of self-awareness, managing emotions, understanding non-verbal cues, and practicing active listening culminate in the ability to express empathy in ways that are authentic and transformative. Let's explore how to make empathy a guiding principle in our relationships:

- **Be an active listener:** The foundation of true empathy is the ability to listen deeply and without judgment. Practicing the active listening skills we've discussed empowers us to genuinely connect with another person's experience.
- **Offer advice... only when asked:** While our intention to help might be noble, unsolicited advice can feel dismissive of someone's pain. Empathy fosters respect for their journey, trusting they have wisdom within themselves. Simple phrases like "This sounds so difficult for you" convey support without trying to take ownership of their problem.
- **Provide emotional and physical comfort:** The way we offer support matters. A caring touch or simply offering our presence can convey understanding deeper than words. Empathy helps us be attuned to what the other person needs, and whether offering practical help or just quiet companionship is most appropriate.
- **Validate the person's experience:** Telling someone to "get over it" or to "look on the bright side" invalidates their feelings. Empathy teaches us that even if we haven't had the same experience, we can acknowledge their emotions

as real and important. Example: "It makes sense that you're angry about what happened. That would make anyone feel angry."

- **Be patient:** Empathy is a journey, not a destination. There will be times you get it wrong or feel unsure of how to respond. Self-compassion allows you to learn from these moments without shame. It motivates you to keep improving rather than giving up on connecting empathically with those you care about.

Like any skillset, mastery in communication and empathy comes through consistent practice. Don't get discouraged if these changes don't feel natural at first. Seek out everyday opportunities to consciously choose your words, observe non-verbal cues, truly listen to others, and express genuine empathy. Each conversation becomes a chance to strengthen your EI muscles. With dedication, you'll transform not only how you interact with others, but also how you understand yourself, leading to deeper, more fulfilling relationships in all spheres of your life.

COMMON TIPS FOR EFFECTIVE COMMUNICATION ACROSS RELATIONSHIPS

There are several universal principles that enhance communication across all aspects of our lives. Whether connecting with a romantic partner, resolving a family issue, or collaborating with a colleague, these foundational skills pave the way for understanding, empathy, and successful problem-solving.

- **Be fully present:** Put away distractions and give the person your undivided attention whenever possible. This shows respect and fosters deeper listening. (EI connection: self-regulation, focus, respect.)

- **Choose your words carefully:** Think before you speak, especially in emotionally charged situations. This reduces the likelihood of saying something hurtful. (EI connection: self-awareness, self-regulation, empathy.)
- **Practice active listening:** Focus on truly understanding the other person's perspective. Reflect back what you hear, ask clarifying questions, and validate their feelings. (EI connection: empathy, focus, non-judgmental stance.)
- **Use "I" statements:** Express your own feelings and needs without blaming the other person. This makes communication less defensive and more solution-oriented. (EI connection: self-awareness, empathy, mindful communication.)
- **Seek to understand, not just to be understood:** Ask open-ended questions and truly listen to the other person's perspective, even if you disagree. (EI connection: empathy, humility.)
- **Be willing to compromise:** Healthy relationships often involve finding solutions that honor everyone's needs. (EI connection: flexibility, understanding others' needs.)
- **Own your mistakes:** If you misunderstand or say something hurtful, taking responsibility helps repair trust. (EI connection: self-awareness, taking responsibility.)
- **Focus on the positive:** Regularly express appreciation and gratitude to build a foundation of positivity in the relationship. (EI connection: optimism, fostering a positive emotional atmosphere.)

SPECIFIC TIPS BY RELATIONSHIP TYPE

While mastering the fundamentals of communication is essential, it's equally important to recognize the subtle nuances that exist within different types of relationships. Romantic partners, families, friends, and workplace colleagues all have unique dynamics. Tailoring your communication approach to each context further strengthens these bonds.

Romantic Relationships

- **Set aside dedicated time for connection, especially for difficult conversations.** This creates a space for uninterrupted communication and shows respect for the importance of the conversation. (EI connection: prioritizing the relationship, respect.)
- **Express physical affection in a way that's meaningful to your partner.** Non-verbal communication demonstrates emotional connection and care. (EI connection: understanding your partner's needs, empathy.)
- **Learn and respect each other's communication styles and preferences.** Adapting your communication style shows empathy and fosters a sense of being heard and understood. (EI connection: empathy, flexibility.)

Family

- **Hold regular family meetings.** This provides a structured forum for open communication and addressing issues proactively. (EI connection: proactive approach, respect for everyone's time.)
- **Establish clear expectations and boundaries.** This reduces confusion and promotes a sense of security and trust within the family unit. (EI connection: understanding needs, clarity in communication.)

- **Celebrate family traditions.** This creates shared positive memories and strengthens the family bond. (EI connection: fostering a sense of belonging, shared positive experiences.)

Parent-Child

- **Model the communication skills you want your child to adopt.** Children learn by observing—demonstrate the skills you hope to see in them. (EI connection: self-awareness, influencing by example.)
- **Adjust your communication to match your child's developmental stage.** Tailoring your approach ensures your child understands and feels heard. (EI connection: empathy, flexibility.)
- **Be patient and consistent.** Building strong communication takes time and consistent effort. (EI connection: self-regulation, commitment to long-term goals.)

Friendships

- **Make time for regular connection.** This shows that you value the friendship and are invested in maintaining it. (EI connection: valuing relationships.)
- **Be genuinely supportive.** Offer emotional support during difficult times and celebrate their successes. (EI connection: empathy, understanding.)
- **Be forgiving.** Everyone makes mistakes—understanding this will foster stronger friendships. (EI connection: empathy, understanding that everyone makes mistakes.)

Workplace

- **Communicate expectations clearly and in a timely manner.** This reduces confusion and ensures everyone is on the same page. (EI connection: clarity, respect for others' time.)
- **Provide constructive feedback with a focus on growth and improvement.** Helps colleagues develop their skills while maintaining a positive working relationship. (EI connection: empathy, mindful communication.)
- **Seek out opportunities to collaborate.** This demonstrates an understanding of the value of teamwork. (EI connection: understanding the value of teamwork.)

By actively applying these communication strategies, you'll cultivate greater understanding, respect, and empathy within all your relationships. However, even with the best intentions, conflicts and misunderstandings are an inevitable part of life. EI provides the tools to navigate these challenges with grace and resilience.

NAVIGATING RELATIONSHIP CHALLENGES WITH EI

Disagreements and challenges are an inevitable part of any relationship. While every situation is unique, there are some common misconceptions that can derail our efforts to navigate conflict constructively. This section explores a few of these myths and offers alternative perspectives informed by EI. By reframing our thinking, we can approach conflict as an opportunity for growth and strengthen the bonds we share.

Myth #1: "Conflict destroys relationships."

- **Why it's harmful:** This myth breeds fear of disagreement. Instead of seeing conflict as a chance for growth, people shut down, problems fester, and resentment builds.
- **EI reframe:** Conflict is an opportunity for deeper understanding and stronger bonds *if* addressed with respect, empathy, and a willingness to find solutions that honor everyone's needs.

Myth #2: "Honesty is always the best policy, no matter how blunt."

- **Why it's harmful:** This approach disregards the importance of empathy and tact. While honesty is vital, how we communicate is equally important. Harsh truths without consideration for the other person's feelings can damage trust.
- **EI reframe:** True honesty combines sincerity with sensitivity. Consider timing, delivery, and the ability to express difficult truths in ways that foster dialogue and minimize defensiveness.

Myth #3: "If they truly care about me, they should just know what I need."

- **Why it's harmful:** This mindset places unrealistic expectations on partners, friends, or family. It sets the stage for resentment when those expectations aren't met.
- **EI reframe:** Even loved ones aren't mind readers. Clear communication of our needs and expectations, along with a willingness to listen to the needs of others, is essential for healthy relationships.

Myth #4: "You can just walk away from an argument."

- **Why it's harmful:** This mindset can lead to avoidance, unresolved issues, and a breakdown in communication. Leaving things hanging can erode trust and create patterns of unresolved conflict within the relationship. Additionally, going to bed in a highly emotional state can disrupt sleep, escalate negative emotions overnight, and make finding a resolution the next day even more challenging.
- **EI reframe:** When possible, it's healthier to work towards a resolution before parting ways. This requires self-regulation, empathy, and a commitment to finding mutually agreeable solutions. However, it's crucial to recognize when it becomes emotionally unproductive to continue. If high emotions risk further harm to the relationship, agree to pause, practice self-soothing, and commit to revisiting the issue with a calmer mindset.

Myth #5: "Relationships shouldn't be hard work."

- **Why it's harmful:** This sets unrealistic expectations. All relationships, even healthy ones, require effort, growth, and adaptation over time. The idea that things should always be effortless breeds disillusionment when inevitable challenges arise.
- **EI reframe:** Healthy relationships involve a willingness to invest effort, compromise, and navigate challenges together. This type of "work" is fueled by love, respect, and a shared commitment. Framing this effort as a positive investment creates a more resilient mindset.

While these tips address some common myths, effective conflict resolution is a nuanced skill. Finding solutions that address everyone's concerns fosters a sense of fairness and strengthens bonds. Remember, open communication and a healthy dose of EI can transform conflict from a destructive force to a catalyst for stronger, more understanding relationships.

Throughout this chapter, we've explored the transformative power of EI in our relationships. From understanding our own emotions to communicating with clarity and empathy, the skills of EI lay the foundation for deeper, more meaningful connections. By actively integrating these principles into your interactions with loved ones, colleagues, and friends, you'll cultivate greater understanding, resilience, and joy in your relationships. However, a fulfilling life isn't solely about relationships. As we navigate life's inevitable ups and downs, our ability to manage stress effectively plays a major role in our overall well-being. Let's turn our attention to this crucial skill in the next chapter.

CHAPTER FIVE

MANAGING STRESS

From the moment we wake up, we're bombarded with an endless stream of information, demands, and expectations. Checking social media, juggling errands, and navigating personal and professional obligations can sometimes feel like an endless struggle to keep up. This chronic pressure takes a toll; it's natural to feel overwhelmed or stressed.

While stress is a common experience, many people don't feel they have adequate resources to manage it properly. The results of the American Psychological Association's (APA) annual survey, *Stress in America 2023: A Nation Recovering from Collective Trauma*, reveal a troubling reality. 61% of people indicated that they felt unsupported in their efforts to manage stress, with many reporting being told to simply "get over it." Nearly half (47%) struggled to find helpful strategies for stress management, with 33% feeling chronically overwhelmed despite their efforts. Over a third (36%) didn't know where to start when managing stress. A strong support system is essential for navigating life's challenges, but two-thirds

(66%) indicated they could have used more emotional support and over half (52%) wished for someone to turn to for advice.

This underscores the importance of providing accessible tools and resources to promote healthy stress management and build supportive communities where people feel comfortable asking for help.

The good news is that you don't have to be a victim of your circumstances. EI provides a powerful toolkit for effectively managing the inevitable stresses of life. This chapter aims to empower you with EI-based strategies to identify your stress triggers, understand their root causes, and regulate your responses. By developing a personalized stress management plan, you can take control, increasing your resilience and overall well-being.

STRESS AND ITS IMPACT

Stress is a natural part of the human experience. It's a complex response involving both our body and mind, designed to help us cope with challenges, perceived threats, or situations where we feel out of control. The causes of stress can be highly personal, but here are some common scenarios where it might arise:

- Personal Challenges: When life feels overwhelming with personal responsibilities, deadlines, or difficult decisions, it's natural to feel stressed.
- Group Stress: If your family, your group of friends, or another close-knit community is facing difficulties like loss, conflict, or financial hardship, these pressures can create a shared sense of stress.
- Community-Wide Stress: Being part of a group that experiences discrimination, injustice, or other forms of adversity can trigger stress for everyone involved.

- Widespread Stress: Major events like natural disasters, pandemics, or societal changes can create stress on a large scale. It's important to remember that even when people experience the same stressful event, their individual reactions can differ greatly.

Recognizing when stress starts to become a problem is the first step towards managing it. In small doses, it can be helpful, giving us a burst of energy and focus to tackle a deadline or overcome an obstacle. However, when stress becomes chronic or overwhelming, it can wreak havoc on our well-being.

Let's break down the two main types of stress:

- **Acute Stress:** This is the intense but short-lived jolt of adrenaline you feel before a presentation or during a sudden unexpected event. It typically fades within minutes or hours as the immediate stressor passes.
- **Chronic Stress:** Unlike acute stress, this feels like a persistent burden that weighs on you for weeks, months, or even years. It can come from ongoing sources like work pressures, financial worries, difficult relationships, or health concerns.

Chronic stress isn't just emotionally draining; it takes a serious toll on both our physical and mental health. Our bodies were not designed for constant stress. When pressures persist, hormones like cortisol flood our system, leading to a cascade of negative effects. For example, chronic stress can contribute to mental health challenges, like anxiety, depression, difficulty concentrating, and problems with memory. You might find yourself feeling overwhelmed, irritable, or constantly on edge. The long-term effects of stress can also manifest physically, in the form of headaches, muscle tension, digestive issues, high blood pressure, heart disease, sleep problems, and a weakened immune system.

By detecting the early signs of stress and understanding its impact, we can take proactive steps to manage it effectively. EI plays a crucial role in this process.

THE ROLE OF EI IN IDENTIFYING STRESS CAUSES AND TRIGGERS

EI can help you better understand and manage your emotions and reactions. By paying attention to the emotions that arise in specific situations, you can start to connect the dots between external events and your internal stress response. This self-awareness can guide you towards identifying the root causes of your stress—and those situations that seem to reliably trigger those stress reactions. Additionally, EI allows you to recognize unhealthy thought patterns or self-talk that might exacerbate feelings of stress, enabling you to choose better coping mechanisms.

Stress triggers are situations, events, thoughts, or even people that consistently provoke a stress response within you. It's important to remember that what causes one individual significant stress might be completely manageable for another. Here are some common types of stressors to consider:

- **Emotional:** Feeling overwhelmed, anxious, fearful, sad, angry, frustrated, guilty, ashamed, or having low self-esteem. These negative emotions can be triggered by internal factors (e.g., perfectionism, procrastination) or external situations (e.g., conflict with a loved one).
- **Environmental:** Our surroundings can significantly impact our stress levels. Factors like noise pollution, clutter, uncomfortable temperatures, poor air quality,

toxins, crowds, and overstimulation can all trigger stress responses.

- **Work-Related:** The workplace can be a breeding ground for stress. Excessive workload, tight deadlines, conflicting demands, lack of control, unclear expectations, difficult colleagues, job insecurity, and lack of recognition can all contribute to feeling overwhelmed and stressed.
- **Technological Stressors:** Information overload, constant connectivity, dependence on technology, and fear of missing out (FOMO) can all contribute to stress, especially for younger generations.
- **Time Management Stress:** Feeling overwhelmed or out of control due to a busy schedule, conflicting commitments, or procrastination can be a stressor.
- **Social:** Navigating social interactions can be stressful, especially for those with social anxiety or a fear of judgment. Conflict, pressure to conform, strained relationships, isolation, and unhealthy comparisons (especially fueled by social media) can all be sources of stress.
- **Life Changes:** Major life transitions are inevitable, and the uncertainty and disruption they bring can be stressful. Events like a new job, moving, marriage, divorce, birth of a child, or death of a loved one can all trigger stress responses.
- **Decision Overload:** Facing significant choices, whether related to career paths, relationships, or major purchases, can be paralyzing. Feeling pressured to make the right decision and the fear of making a mistake can be significant sources of stress.
- **Financial Stressors:** These include debt, job insecurity, unexpected bills, and difficulty affording basic needs.

Financial worries are a significant source of stress for many people.

- **Chemical Stressors:** Certain substances, when used excessively, can disrupt our body's natural balance and contribute to stress. These include caffeine, nicotine, alcohol, and recreational drugs.
- **Health-Related:** Disruptions to our physical well-being can be major stressors. This includes lack of sleep, poor nutrition, dehydration, illness, and side effects of medication. Additionally, chronic illness and undergoing medical procedures can also contribute to stress.
- **Pain:** Both acute and chronic pain can be significant stressors. Acute pain from an injury and the ongoing challenges of managing chronic pain conditions can take a toll on our well-being.
- **Sensory Overload:** For individuals with sensory processing sensitivities, loud noises, bright lights, strong smells, or crowded environments can be particularly stressful.

Take a few moments now to reflect on the different types of stressors mentioned above. Jot down the ones that resonate with you, and try to pinpoint specific situations or experiences that reliably lead to feelings of stress. Having this list handy will be incredibly valuable as you continue working through this chapter.

How Stress Triggers Work: A Chain Reaction

When you encounter a stress trigger, it sets off a chain reaction within your body. Here's a breakdown of the process:

1. **Perception:** Your brain perceives a situation or event as potentially threatening or challenging.

2. **Hormonal Response:** The amygdala, your body's "fight-or-flight" center, triggers the release of hormones like adrenaline and cortisol.
3. **Physical Changes:** This hormonal surge increases your heart rate, breathing rate, and blood pressure, preparing your body to react quickly.
4. **Emotional Response:** You might experience feelings of anxiety, frustration, anger, or fear alongside the physical changes.

Understanding how your body reacts to stress triggers is the crucial first step for effectively managing them. By recognizing the early warning signs—the physical sensations, emotions, and thoughts that arise—you can take proactive steps to manage the stress cycle before it escalates.

Self-Reflection: Decoding Your Stress

EI empowers you to become an expert on your own stress responses. Consider turning these questions into journal prompts for a deeper dive into your unique stress triggers and how to manage them. Reflecting on the following questions can provide valuable insights:

- **Warning Signs:** What physical (e.g., headaches, rapid heartbeat), mental (e.g., racing thoughts, difficulty focusing), and emotional (e.g., anger, sadness, worry) changes signal to you that stress is building?
- **Stress Sensations:** Describe in detail the physical and emotional sensations you experience when stressed.
- **Timing and Triggers:** Are there specific times of day, days of the week, or situations where you're more likely to feel stressed? Can you identify your top three stressors?

Why do you think these situations trigger a stress response?

- **Intensity and Impact:** On a scale of 1–10 (with 10 being extremely stressed), how would you rate the intensity of your stress responses? Does your stress level interfere with your ability to work, socialize, or enjoy your daily life?
- **Coping Strategies:** Do you have healthy ways to manage stress, or do you fall into unhelpful patterns (e.g., emotional eating, isolating yourself)? What techniques or strategies have you tried in the past to manage stress? Were they helpful or unhelpful?
- **Support and Prevention:** Who can you rely on for support when you feel stressed? Are there lifestyle changes, boundaries, or routines you could implement to reduce your baseline stress levels?
- **Moving Toward Change:** Describe a stress-free day in detail. How would you feel? What would you be doing or not doing? What unhelpful habits, commitments, or thought patterns could you release to reduce stress? What is one small, positive change you can make today to move closer to your stress-free vision?

EI's strength lies in its potential to help you manage stress proactively. The following strategies will equip you with the skills needed not only to cope with stressors, but also to strengthen your overall resilience.

Mindfulness & Self-Awareness Practices

- Body Scan: Systematically focus attention on different parts of your body, noticing sensations without judgment. This enhances awareness of physical signs of stress.

- Mindful Breathing: Consciously slow and deepen your breaths, focusing on the sensations of breathing. This activates your parasympathetic nervous system, promoting relaxation (Zaccaro et al., 2018).
- Sensory Grounding: Pay attention to what you can see, hear, smell, feel, and taste in the present moment. This anchors you in the here-and-now, reducing anxiety about the future or rumination on the past.

Emotional Regulation

- Name Your Emotions: Clearly identifying how you're feeling (e.g., "I'm angry," "I'm overwhelmed") helps you gain distance from them and reduces their intensity.
- Reframe Negative Thoughts: Challenge self-critical thoughts, catastrophizing, or all-or-nothing thinking with more balanced perspectives. This prevents unhelpful thinking patterns from amplifying stress.
- Self-Compassion: Treat yourself with the kindness and understanding you'd offer a friend during stressful times. Shame and self-blame can worsen stress and make it harder to cope; self-compassion helps counteract these harmful feelings.
- Time in Nature: Spending time in natural settings has been shown to reduce stress, improve mood, and increase emotional well-being.

Healthy Coping, Boundaries & Mindset Shifts

- Self-Care: Prioritize activities that nourish your physical and mental well-being, such as exercise, nutritious food, and getting enough sleep.

- Set Boundaries: Learn to say "no" to requests that overload you, and practice communicating your needs assertively. This protects your time and resources, reducing overwhelm.
- Seek Social Support: Connect with supportive friends, family members, or a therapist. Sharing your burdens reduces isolation and provides emotional support.
- Practice Gratitude: Focus on the positive aspects of your life. This shifts your perspective, reducing negativity and promoting resilience.
- Address Perfectionism: Strive for excellence, not unattainable perfection. Perfectionism fuels stress; learn to embrace "good enough."
- Challenge the Need for Instant Gratification: Practice delayed gratification and focus on long-term goals. Instant gratification can create a cycle of craving and disappointment, increasing stress levels.
- Reframe Mistakes as Learning Opportunities: Mistakes are an inevitable part of growth. Use them to learn and improve rather than getting stuck in self-blame.

DEVELOPING YOUR STRESS MANAGEMENT PLAN

There's no one-size-fits-all solution for managing stress. By exploring your triggers with reflective questions and considering healthy coping strategies, you've laid the groundwork for a plan that truly addresses your needs. Now, let's turn those insights into a personalized stress management plan, ensuring you're equipped with strategies tailored to your unique stressors, vulnerabilities, and preferences.

Step 1: Unearth Your Triggers

- **Journaling:** Use the provided prompts to reflect on your stress responses. Identify specific situations, thoughts, people, or events that consistently trigger your stress.
- **Look for Patterns:** Analyze your responses. Are there common themes in your stressors? Do they fall into categories like work-related, social, or related to personal insecurities?
- **Underlying Vulnerabilities:** Consider factors that might make you more susceptible to stress. This could include perfectionism, negative self-talk, social anxiety, difficulty setting boundaries, or a tendency to dwell on the past.

Step 2: Build Your Stress-Busting Toolkit

- **In-the-Moment Relief:** Pinpoint activities or practices that effectively calm you down when stressed. This could include deep breathing, exercise, listening to music, spending time with loved ones, taking a short break to focus on something enjoyable, or trying some of these:

  - Instant Vacation: Close your eyes, and visualize yourself in a tranquil place. Engage all your senses —imagine the sights, sounds, smells, and textures that transport you.
  - Get Creative: Express yourself through art, music, writing, or dance. Losing yourself in creativity can be a powerful way to process emotions and shift your focus.
  - Have Some Fun: Allow yourself to laugh. Watch a funny video, tell jokes, or engage in playful activities that bring pure joy.

- **Skill-Building:** Choose specific EI strategies that address your identified triggers and vulnerabilities. For example:

  o Racing Thoughts: Practice mindfulness and meditation.
  o Difficulty Setting Boundaries: Develop assertiveness skills.
  o Self-Criticism: Focus on self-compassion techniques.
  o Negative Outlook: Practice gratitude journaling or deliberately seek out positive experiences, no matter how small.

Step 3: Focus on Prevention

- **Lifestyle Changes:** Analyze your current routines.

  o Sleep: Are you getting enough restorative sleep? Create a relaxing bedtime routine (Chaput et al., 2020).
  o Nutrition: Are you fuelling your body with healthy foods? Choose whole, nutritious options for sustained energy and stable mood. Remember, everyone's body responds to food differently, so pay attention to how specific foods make you feel (Rooney et al., 2013).
  o Movement: Are you moving your body? Incorporate regular exercise into your day—even a brisk walk can be beneficial (Berger, 1994).

- **Boundaries:** Where in your life can you establish healthier boundaries? This includes learning to say "no," delegating tasks, and prioritizing your own needs.

- **Wellness Practices:** Are there specific mind-body practices that resonate with you?

    ○ Active Relaxation: Choose activities like guided meditations to cultivate calm.
    ○ Emotional Release: Find healthy ways to express emotions like journaling, therapy, creative expression, or exercise.
    ○ Letting Go: Practice mindfulness and self-compassion, letting go of what you can't control.

Step 4: Build Your Support Network

- **Identify Your People:** Who offers emotional support during tough times? This could be friends, family, a therapist, or a support group. Nurture these relationships.
- **Accountability Partner:** Consider sharing your plan with someone who can provide encouragement and help you stay on track.

Step 5: Embrace Flexibility

- **Realistic Expectations:** Stress management is a process. Be patient, and don't be afraid to experiment to find what works best for you.
- **Monitoring Progress:** Regularly check in. Is your plan working? Tweak it as needed, ditching what isn't helpful and adding in new strategies.

Remember, your plan is unique to you! This guide is just a starting point—feel free to adapt and personalize it for the best fit.

REAL-LIFE SUCCESS STORIES

It can be helpful to see how others have put EI principles for stress management into action. Theory is powerful, but sometimes seeing real-life examples makes it click. Let's look at a few different examples of how others have navigated stress successfully. These stories might give you new ideas as you personalize your plan.

Case Study 1: Erica—Overcoming Workplace Overload

- **Challenge:** Erica, a high-achieving project manager, felt constantly overwhelmed by her workload. Tight deadlines, conflicting priorities, and a demanding boss left her feeling exhausted, irritable, and fearing burnout.
- **EI Transformation:**

  - Self-Awareness: Erica started journaling about her work-related stressors, recognizing that her perfectionism and difficulty saying "no" contributed to her overload.
  - Assertive Communication: Rather than passively accepting unreasonable demands, she began practicing clear and assertive communication with her boss. She proposed realistic timelines and negotiated priorities.
  - Boundary Setting: Erica blocked off time in her schedule for focused work without interruptions and started delegating tasks where possible.

- **Result:** Erica regained a sense of control over her workload. Her improved communication skills led to more manageable expectations, and her boundaries reduced stress and improved work-life balance.

Case Study 2: Vikram—Managing Personal Anxiety

- **Challenge:** Vikram struggled with persistent anxiety, often triggered by uncertainty and worries about the future. His racing thoughts and physical symptoms (tightness in the chest, restlessness) made it difficult to focus and enjoy daily life.
- **EI Transformation:**

  - Mindfulness Practice: Vikram began incorporating mindfulness meditation into his daily routine. This helped him learn to observe his anxious thoughts and feelings without judgment, reducing their intensity.
  - Self-Compassion: Recognizing that his harsh self-criticism fuelled his anxiety, Vikram practiced self-compassion, treating himself with the same kindness he would offer a friend.
  - Addressing Root Causes: With the support of a therapist, Vikram started exploring the underlying reasons for his anxiety, working through past experiences and developing healthier thought patterns.

- **Result:** Over time, Vikram's anxiety became less debilitating. Mindfulness helped him interrupt cycles of worry, and developing self-compassion decreased the shame and self-blame that worsened his stress.

Case Study 3: Maria and Ben—Improving Relationship Dynamics

- **Challenge:** Maria and her partner, Ben, frequently engaged in heated arguments. Miscommunication, differing expectations, and unresolved resentments led to a cycle of hurt feelings, defensiveness, and withdrawal.
- **EI Transformation:**

    - Active Listening: Maria and Ben committed to practicing active listening, aiming to understand each other's perspectives without interrupting.
    - Emotion Regulation: Before reacting in anger, they learned to pause, identify their emotions, and express them constructively rather than through blaming.
    - Conflict Resolution: They adopted a problem-solving approach to disagreements, focusing on solutions and compromise instead of assigning blame.

- **Result:** Communication improved, and Maria and Ben developed a stronger sense of teamwork. Their improved ability to regulate emotions decreased the intensity of arguments, and their focus on solutions increased their feelings of trust and security in the relationship.

By understanding your stress triggers, developing personalized coping strategies, and building a strategy for stress management, you've laid a strong foundation for navigating life's inevitable stressors with greater ease. Your plan will evolve over time, as you develop and grow. Keep being patient with yourself, continue to experiment to find what works best, and don't hesitate to seek support when needed. Now, let's explore how EI can be applied in even more real-life scenarios, enhancing your relationships, decision-making, and overall well-being.

CHAPTER SIX

EVERYDAY APPLICATION

 "There is no separation of mind and emotions; emotions, thinking, and learning are all linked."

— ERIC JENSEN (2005)

E motions aren't just fleeting feelings—they shape our thoughts, influence our decision-making, and drive our actions. This has ripple effects, coloring our experiences, impacting our self-perception, motivations, and ability to regulate ourselves, leaving a lasting imprint on our overall well-being. Furthermore, emotions radiate outwards, affecting how we communicate, how we're perceived, and shaping the very nature of our relationships.

This chapter provides you with the tools to harness the power of EI for a more intentional and fulfilling life. Discover practical strategies to integrate EI into your daily routines, fostering greater self-awareness, stronger relationships, and improved adaptability in your inner and interpersonal world.

EXERCISES: FOUR PILLARS OF EI

Building a strong foundation in EI takes dedicated practice. Specific exercises tailored to four of the core pillars—self-awareness, self-regulation, empathy, and social skills—offer powerful tools to navigate life's complexities. These techniques will empower you to understand and manage your emotions with greater clarity and intention.

Self-Awareness

- **The "Who Am I?" Exercise:** This writing exercise, inspired by Carl Rogers' work on self-concept (1995), prompts deep reflection on your identity. Create a list of 20 statements that answer the question "Who am I?" Consider your values, personality traits, roles you occupy, priorities, strengths, and areas for growth. Analyze discrepancies between your aspirational self and how you currently spend your time and energy. This reveals areas where your actions aren't aligned with your self-image, highlights unconscious motivations and beliefs driving your behavior, and sparks the rediscovery of dormant passions or values. You can track your personal evolution over time by periodically repeating the exercise.

- **The Metaphorical Mirror:** This is a creative writing approach to self-examination. Craft a short story or poem centered on a fictional character, embedding elements of your personality, struggles, and aspirations within them. Distance yourself from your direct identity to analyze these traits through a fictional lens. Journal about insights that arise during and after the writing process. This provides a less confrontational way to explore difficult emotions or behaviors, reveals patterns you might miss when only directly analyzing yourself, and encourages creative expression as a tool for self-discovery.

- **The Emotional Soundtrack:** Drawing from music therapy principles, explore the connection between music, emotions, and self. Choose a song with strong emotional resonance for you, positive or negative. Close your eyes and listen deeply, letting the music guide your thoughts and feelings. Journal about the memories, themes, desires, or anxieties the song evokes. This helps identify links between specific emotions and your life experiences, uncovers hidden desires, fears, or unresolved emotions lurking below the surface, and offers an alternative form of self-exploration for people who struggle with traditional journaling.

Self-Regulation

- **The Balloon Breath:** This simple breathing technique that draws from the extensive body of work around the benefits of mindful breathing for both physical and emotional wellbeing, helps manage stress and tension. Inhale slowly through your nose, imagining your belly inflating like a balloon. Hold your breath for a comfortable count of two. Exhale slowly through your mouth, visualizing the balloon deflating and releasing tension. Repeat for several minutes, focusing on the sensation of rising and falling tension. This provides quick stress relief, making it ideal for use anywhere, anytime. It teaches the connection between mindful breathing and emotional state and can be combined with visualization for enhanced calming effects.
- **The Mountain Pose:** This posture-based exercise promotes feelings of inner strength and stability. Stand with your feet

hip-width apart and toes pointing slightly outward. Engage your core muscles and lengthen your spine. Relax your shoulders and arms by your sides. Close your eyes and envision yourself as a sturdy mountain, rooted to the ground and unfazed by external challenges. Hold the pose for several minutes, focusing on your breath and sense of stability. This promotes feelings of being grounded and unshakable in the face of stress, requires focus (disrupting anxious thoughts), and can be combined with affirmations for added impact.

- **Progressive Muscle Relaxation (PMR):** Developed by Edmund Jacobson (1938), this systematic approach to relaxation involves tensing and releasing different muscle groups. Find a quiet, comfortable place to lie down or sit. Begin by tensing and relaxing a specific muscle group, starting with your toes and gradually working your way up your body. Tense the muscles for a few seconds, noticing the sensation, then release them completely, focusing on the feeling of relaxation that follows. Repeat with each muscle group, allowing your body to become progressively more relaxed. PMR reduces anxiety and stress, improves sleep quality, helps manage chronic pain, and builds awareness of your body's stress responses.

Social Skills

- **Role-Playing:** Simulate social scenarios in a safe, controlled environment. Work with a partner or small group to act out challenging conversations or interactions. Start with simple scenarios and gradually increase difficulty. Switch roles to gain different perspectives and provide constructive feedback to each other. This provides a "practice space" to develop conversational skills and confidence, builds situational awareness, and fosters empathy.

- **Speed Friending:** Structured events promote quick, focused interactions with new people. Engage in a series of short, timed conversations with multiple people with some varied topics as prompts. Pay attention to both your own and others' communication styles. This helps overcome social anxiety, improves your ability to make introductions and engage in small talk, and allows you to observe a variety of social skills.

- **Observation and Mimicry:** Learn social skills by observing effective communicators both in real life and through media. Notice their body language, tone of voice, word choice, and the way they manage conversations. Subtly incorporate positive elements of their communication style into your own interactions. This offers a non-intimidating way to learn from positive role models, helps you identify specific behaviors to adapt and practice, and makes you more aware of your own communication patterns.

Empathy

- **The Empathy Gap Interview:** Interview someone about a significant experience, focusing on reflecting their emotions back to them. Choose a partner willing to share a personal experience. Practice actively listening, asking clarifying questions, and reflecting the emotions you hear expressed (verbally and nonverbally). Avoid offering advice or inserting your own experiences during this process. Switch roles so both partners feel deeply listened to. This enhances your ability to identify and understand the emotions of others, improves active listening and mirroring skills, and promotes deeper connections.

- **The Facial Expression Game:** This interactive exercise, inspired by the work of Paul Ekman (1999), a pioneer in the study of facial expressions and emotions, helps recognize and understand emotions expressed through facial cues. Find a set of images clearly depicting different emotions (joy, sadness, anger, fear, etc.). Individually or in a group, attempt to accurately identify and label the emotion portrayed in each image. Discuss what specific facial features led you to your conclusion. This improves your ability to accurately read nonverbal cues, builds a vocabulary of emotions, and can be a fun and engaging way to learn about emotions.

- **The "Dear Abby" Letter:** Imagine yourself as an advice columnist and write a compassionate response to a fictional situation. Think of a hypothetical person struggling with a difficult situation and put yourself in their shoes. Write a letter from the perspective of a compassionate advice columnist, offering support and understanding. This promotes perspective-taking, deepens your ability to identify with the experiences of others, helps you articulate empathy through language, and encourages a mindset of compassion.

These targeted exercises have equipped you with strategies to enhance your overall EI across these four pillars, providing a foundation to put your newfound skills into practice across various life scenarios.

EXERCISES: SPECIFIC SCENARIOS

Building on this foundation, we'll now explore exercises designed to navigate specific scenarios you might encounter in your personal or professional life. These techniques will further empower you to respond with emotional agility and effectiveness, no matter the circumstances.

Work

- **"Pre-mortem Analysis" for Projects:** Before starting a project, imagine it has already failed and brainstorm the reasons why. Then, take steps to proactively address those potential pitfalls. This exercise, inspired by risk management techniques and popularized by psychologist Gary Klein (2004), helps build emotional foresight by anticipating potential frustrations and proactively developing solutions.
- **Assertiveness Scripts:** Before a difficult conversation, write out what you'd like to say. This allows you to manage your own emotions in the moment and ensures you communicate effectively and professionally, even in challenging situations. This exercise has roots in assertiveness training, a component of cognitive behavioral therapy (CBT).
- **Seek Feedback, Mentorship:** Actively ask for feedback on your work performance and seek out a mentor who models good emotional intelligence. This provides valuable insights into your work-specific blind spots and offers a model for how to develop your own EI skills in a professional context.

Relationships

- **Active Listening Practice:** Set aside dedicated time with loved ones without any distractions. Focus on what they are saying, both verbally and nonverbally. This strengthens your ability to be fully present, builds understanding, and deepens your connection.
- **Relationship Review:** Regularly assess the emotional health of important relationships. Consider what dynamics are working well, what challenges you face, and how your own emotional intelligence could positively impact the relationship.
- **Conflict Role-Play:** Practice handling difficult relationship conversations with a trusted friend or partner. Focus on approaching the role-play with empathy and a solution-oriented mindset. This provides a safe space to develop your conflict resolution skills.

Stressful Situations

- **The "5 Senses" Grounding Technique:** When feeling stressed or overwhelmed, focus on five things you can see, four things you can touch, three things you can hear, two things you can smell, and one thing you can taste. This simple practice, that draws from mindfulness practices, helps redirect your attention from emotional overwhelm towards the present moment.
- **The "STOP" Technique:** This acronym stands for Stop, Take a breath, Observe, and Proceed. It's a quick and easy tool to break the cycle of reactivity and introduce an element of self-regulation during stressful moments. This aligns with principles of dialectical behavior therapy

(DBT), a therapy focused on emotional regulation and distress tolerance.

- **Visualized Safe Space:** Picture a place that makes you feel calm and secure. Practice mentally transporting yourself to this safe space during moments of stress, allowing it to provide a quick emotional reset.

Challenging Conversations

- **The Fog Technique:** When facing verbal aggression or unreasonable criticism, avoid defending yourself or escalating the situation. Instead, respond with neutral, non-engaging statements or even agree in part with the criticism (if applicable). This helps to diffuse the situation and protects your emotional well-being.
- **"Feel, Felt, Found":** Use this structure to give feedback constructively: "I feel [emotion] when [situation occurs]. Others have felt the same. I found [a solution/alternative approach]". This frames feedback in a way that focuses on the impact of the situation and potential solutions.
- **"I" Statements:** Take ownership of your feelings during disagreements by using "I" language (e.g.: "I feel hurt when...") instead of accusatory "You" statements. This helps to de-escalate conflict and focuses on expressing your own experience rather than placing blame.

Grief and Loss:

- **Guided Journaling with Prompts:** Use specific prompts designed to explore emotions surrounding loss and change. Questions like "What am I mourning alongside the person/situation?" or "What do I wish I'd said?" guide the process.

- **Legacy Projects:** Work on something that honors the person or thing you've lost—a scrapbook, a memorial garden, etc. This channels grief into a constructive and meaningful activity.
- **Mindfulness for Grief:** Focus on the present moment with techniques like body scans. This acknowledges grief without being overwhelmed.

Health-Related Concerns:

- **Progressive Muscle Relaxation for Scans/Procedures:** Exercise PMR before potentially stressful moments like medical tests (Jacobson, 1938).
- **"Worry Time" Exercise:** Limit worrying to a short "appointment" per day. During it, write down every worry, then consciously put it aside for later, freeing your mind for the present.
- **The Impermanence Meditation:** This focuses on how everything changes, including difficult emotions and health states. It's helpful against the fear that things may never be okay again.

Major Life Transitions:

- **The Values Check-in:** When major choices loom (new job, moving, etc.), write down your core values. Then, assess how each option aligns with them to reduce decision fatigue. This aligns with acceptance and commitment therapy (ACT) concepts, which emphasize values-driven living.
- **The Positive Possibilities List:** Alongside practical concerns, make a list of hopes and dreams related to the

change. This cultivates some excitement alongside the uncertainty.

- **"Future Self" Letter:** Write a letter to yourself a year ahead. Imagine you've adjusted well and things are good; focus on how you got there and the strength it took.

Caregiving Responsibilities:

- **Mindful Breaks:** Even five minutes of focusing on your breath or a pleasant sensory experience provides a much-needed "reset" amidst overwhelming care duties.
- **Support Network Map:** Chart out all forms of help you could theoretically access—practical, emotional, respite care. It helps battle the "I have to do it all alone" feeling.
- **The "One Good Thing" Reflection:** End each day noting at least one positive occurrence, no matter how small, to combat burnout.

Financial Stress:

- **The "Needs vs. Wants" Audit:** Reviewing spending habits offers clarity, reducing the generalized anxiety that comes with financial distress.
- **Gratitude Practice for Non-Material Things:** Focus on the good aspects of your life that cost nothing. This counters the feeling that finances determine your happiness.
- **"Information Hour":** Set aside time for learning about budgeting, debt relief, etc. Taking action lessens the helpless feeling often accompanying financial strain.

Boosting Motivation

- **Small Goal Setting:** Break down large, overwhelming goals into manageable daily or weekly tasks. This helps maintain motivation by building self-efficacy through visible progress.
- **The "Why Ladder":** If you're struggling with a lack of purpose, ask yourself "Why is this task important?" Continue asking "why" until you reach a core motivating value that drives you. This has parallels to motivational interviewing techniques.
- **Visualization of Success:** Before taking on something difficult, vividly imagine yourself achieving your desired outcome and the positive feelings of success. This helps boost motivation and confidence.

Take a moment now to reflect on the challenges you face most often. Which exercises seem like a good fit to help you navigate them? Continue to build on your EI toolkit with a short list of your go-to strategies.

ESTABLISHING EI-ENHANCING HABITS

To truly integrate EI into your life, consider adopting daily habits that promote ongoing self-awareness, emotional regulation, empathy and social fluency:

- **Mindfulness Practice:** Even a few minutes of daily mindfulness exercises—such as focused breathing or a body scan—strengthens your ability to stay grounded and present in the face of stress.
- **Emotional Check-ins:** Schedule regular "check-ins" with yourself to observe your current emotional state. This

promotes self-awareness and allows you to proactively
address feelings before they become overwhelming.

- **Setting Intentions for EI Regulation:** At the start of your
  day, or before a challenging situation, set a clear intention
  for how you want to respond emotionally (e.g., "I will stay
  calm during difficult conversations"). This primes your
  mind for better self-regulation.
- **Perspective-Taking:** Actively seek out viewpoints
  different from your own. Read articles you disagree with,
  watch documentaries on unfamiliar lives, or engage in
  respectful debate with someone who holds opposing
  views. This promotes empathy and challenges your own
  assumptions.
- **Enhanced Emotional Vocabulary and Thought
  Awareness:** Pay attention to how you name your emotions
  and the internal dialogue that accompanies them. Learning
  to identify specific emotions (e.g., feeling frustrated
  instead of simply "bad"), and their corresponding thought
  patterns ("I'll never get this right" vs. "This is a challenge I
  can overcome"), provides greater clarity for challenging
  unhelpful thoughts.
- **Forgive Yourself and Practice Self-Compassion:**
  Cultivate kindness towards yourself, especially during
  difficult moments. Acknowledge mistakes without harsh
  self-judgment, fostering a sense of self-acceptance.
- **Continuous Learning About EI:** Dedicate even a small
  amount of time daily to learning about different aspects of
  EI. This could involve reading articles, listening to
  podcasts, or exploring the exercises in this book.

Start small and focus on what you can realistically fit into your life.
Choose one or two exercises to focus on initially, ensuring they fit
realistically within your current lifestyle. This sets you up for

success and prevents feeling overwhelmed. It's also crucial to find practices that resonate with you—if journaling feels forced, explore alternative self-reflection methods or focus on building your mindfulness or perspective-taking skills. The more you enjoy the process, the easier it will be to stay consistent.

Consistency is key, so find ways to track your progress. This could involve keeping a journal specifically for your EI development or utilizing a habit-tracking app. Seeing your progress, even those small initial victories, will boost your motivation. Celebrate those milestones! Reward yourself with something that reinforces the positive journey you're on.

Another helpful strategy is habit stacking. This involves attaching a new EI-enhancing habit to an existing routine. For example, you could try a five-minute journaling practice with your morning coffee or do a quick mindful breathing exercise while brushing your teeth. This leverages the power of established habits to create a "cue" for the new behavior you want to solidify.

Finally, remember that flexibility is important. If a particular practice stops working for you, don't view it as a failure. Instead, be willing to adapt. Experiment with different approaches or focus on other areas of EI until you find what aligns best with your current needs.

NAVIGATING SOCIAL SITUATIONS WITH EI

The journey of developing emotional intelligence starts inwards. Understanding your own emotions and developing healthy coping mechanisms has given you a strong foundation for the next big step: social interactions.

Social situations present a unique set of challenges. Reading non-verbal cues, understanding unspoken messages, and managing your own emotional responses in the presence of others requires a different skillset. Here are some practical tips to help you sharpen your social EI skills and move from a place of self-management to effective social interaction:

Reading the Room

- **Learn to read nonverbal cues:** Pay attention to body language, facial expressions, and tone of voice. These often reveal more about how a person or group is feeling than their actual words.
- **Stay out of your head:** Avoid overthinking or assuming you know what others are thinking. Focus on the observable cues they project instead of your internal interpretations.
- **Practice reading between the lines:** Consider the context of a situation, indirect phrasing, and hints within a conversation. This helps you understand the full meaning behind what's said.
- **Ask for feedback:** If unsure about the social dynamics, confide in a trusted friend or colleague to get their perspective. Sometimes, an outside view helps clarify things.
- **Don't forget about basic needs:** Fatigue, hunger, or discomfort can make anyone irritable. Factor in these basic needs when gauging a social situation—sometimes the mood of the room can shift with a simple snack break!

Managing Emotional Responses

- **Consider your emotions without judging them:** If you feel overwhelmed or triggered, acknowledge the feeling without labeling it "good" or "bad." Simply naming your emotion can start the regulation process.

- **Look at things from a different point of view:** Actively attempt to see a situation from someone else's perspective. This promotes empathy and de-escalates reactive responses.
- **Replace negative thoughts with positive ones:** Challenge unhelpful thought patterns ("They don't like me") with more realistic ones ("I'm new here, and it takes time to build connections").
- **Be kind to yourself:** Social situations can be stressful! If you make a faux pas, extend yourself the same compassion you'd give a friend.

Mindful Pause Before Reacting

- **Recognize the trigger:** What specific behavior or statement caused your emotional reaction? Identifying the trigger is key to managing it effectively.
- **Press pause:** Don't react on impulse. Give yourself a short mental break, even just a few seconds.
- **Take a deep breath:** A single conscious breath activates your parasympathetic nervous system, promoting a sense of calm.
- **Observe:** Step back mentally and observe the situation more objectively, including your own feelings.
- **Press play:** Respond from a more collected and thoughtful place, rather than reacting on autopilot.

Social skills, like any EI skill, are strengthened through practice. Embrace opportunities for interaction, observe, learn, and continue to refine your ability to navigate the social world with both emotional awareness and effectiveness. By consciously applying these tips, you increase your understanding of others, express yourself more effectively, and build stronger, more meaningful connections.

This chapter explored how various approaches, from self-reflection exercises to mindfulness techniques and strategies for navigating social scenarios, can equip you to understand and manage your emotions with greater effectiveness. You've gained a practical understanding of EI and its impact on your personal growth. Next, you'll learn how to harness self-awareness, emotional regulation, empathy, and social skills to approach life's challenges with a strengthened sense of inner resourcefulness.

CHAPTER SEVEN

OVERCOMING OBSTACLES

Have you ever found yourself locked in a battle to be right, or felt frustrated when others don't seem to understand your feelings? Maybe you sometimes feel overwhelmed by challenges, find yourself blaming outside factors when things go wrong, or struggle to let go of past mistakes? We all experience these moments, and recognizing them within ourselves is an important step towards personal growth and a sign of strong self-awareness. It's in these situations where developing our EI can make a major difference in our lives.

Even when we recognize the benefits and importance of stronger EI, it's natural to encounter moments of skepticism, struggle to find time for practice, or experience resistance to change. Understanding these and other potential roadblocks is crucial for navigating them effectively. Think of it like planning a hike—knowing about potential challenges, like changing terrain or unexpected weather, helps you prepare accordingly. Similarly, by recognizing the obstacles you might face in developing your EI, you can actively work to address them.

This chapter addresses these common challenges and explores the typical hurdles and misconceptions that might hold you back. You'll discover practical strategies to overcome skepticism, integrate EI practices into your busy life, and break through resistance to change.

CONFRONTING SKEPTICISM AND DOUBT

A healthy dose of skepticism keeps us curious and encourages us to seek deeper understanding. However, persistent doubt can prevent you from fully embracing the potential of EI to transform your life.

Let's tackle some of the most common misconceptions around EI. We'll also share strategies to address them, so you can move forward without reservations.

Misconception #1—Lack of Understanding: EI is about being nice and charismatic. It's a "soft skill" that doesn't translate into tangible results in the workplace or personal life.

- **Reframe:** This view reduces EI to superficial personality traits and ignores the fact that it encompasses a wide range of essential skills, including self-awareness, empathy, and self-regulation. Far from being a "soft skill," EI is directly linked to improved work performance, stronger interpersonal relationships, and greater overall well-being.

Misconception #2—Difficulty Measuring Outcomes: EI development doesn't have standardized measures like traditional IQ tests, making it seem less scientific or impactful.

- **Reframe:** While measuring EI has its complexities, research tools and assessments, like the Mayer-Salovey-Caruso Emotional Intelligence Test (MSCEIT) and the Emotional and Social Competency Inventory (ESCI), help track progress. The MSCEIT offers an ability-based measure of EI, while the ESCI, which is particularly valuable for leadership development and workplace settings, uses observer ratings. Alongside these assessments, real-life, qualitative indicators, like stronger relationships and improved decision-making skills, also provide evidence of growth.

Misconception #3—Focus on No Short-Term Gains: EI development requires ongoing effort and doesn't produce immediate, noticeable benefits. This leads to discouragement.

- **Reframe:** EI development is a journey of continuous growth. Consistent practice leads to subtle, positive changes that compound over time, resulting in significant transformations. Think of it like planting a seed—you won't see the mature plant overnight, but with consistent care, it will eventually grow and bear fruit.

Misconception #4—Negative Past Experiences: Exposure to poorly executed EI training or superficial techniques can create a negative association with the concept.

- **Reframe:** Effective EI development goes beyond surface-level tactics and focuses on deep understanding and integration for sustainable growth. Unfortunately, some programs oversimplify EI or focus on short-term behavior modification. Seek out training that emphasizes self-reflection, skill-building exercises, and the science behind EI's impact, empowering you to make lasting changes.

Misconception #5—Belief in Fixed Traits: EI is a fixed trait, rather than a skill that can be developed.

- **Reframe:** Neuroscience reveals that our brains have a remarkable ability to change and adapt throughout life, with the capacity to form new connections and pathways, called neuroplasticity (Kaczmarek, 2020). This means that with intentional practice and learning, you can strengthen the neural pathways that support EI skills. While some people might have a natural head start, everyone has the potential to significantly improve their emotional intelligence.

With a better understanding of EI's true potential, let's explore how to overcome challenges and make it a transformative part of your life. We'll look at practical strategies for a busy lifestyle, and techniques to navigate resistance for lasting growth.

EI DEVELOPMENT FOR THE BUSY INDIVIDUAL

Let's start with some simple, time-friendly exercises that you can easily fit into your day, no matter how hectic it may be.

- One-Line-a-Day Gratitude Journaling (one minute): Take 60 seconds at the end of your day to quickly jot down one thing you're grateful for. This simple act of intentionally focusing on the positive fosters a more optimistic mindset and a greater appreciation for the good in your life.
- One-Minute Breathwork (one minute): Find a quiet spot, close your eyes, and focus on your breath. Inhale for a

count of 4, hold for 4, and exhale for a count of 8. Repeat this cycle four times. This practice calms the mind, reducing feelings of stress and anxiety while improving emotional regulation.

- One-Minute Meditation (one minute): Find a comfortable seated position and close your eyes. Focus on your breath as it flows in and out of your body, gently bringing your attention back to it whenever your mind wanders. This practice develops mindfulness, a key component of emotional intelligence that helps you remain present and non-judgmental of your own thoughts and feelings.

- Label It, Don't Judge It (two minutes): When a difficult emotion arises, take a moment to name it without judgment. For example, "I feel frustrated right now." Simply identifying the emotion allows you to step back slightly from it, lessening its intensity and promoting self-awareness.

- Quick Body Scan (two minutes): Close your eyes and focus on your physical sensations. Scan different areas of your body, noticing any tension or tightness. This practice enhances your ability to recognize how your emotions manifest physically, which promotes self-regulation and stress management.

- Positive Affirmations (two minutes): Choose a positive affirmation that resonates with you, such as "I am calm and capable." Repeat it silently or aloud a few times. Affirmations work by consciously replacing negative or limiting self-talk with positive beliefs, which impacts how you feel and behave.

Consistency is vital when building the habit of practicing EI. By incorporating these simple exercises into your routine, you'll start to notice subtle yet meaningful shifts in your awareness, mindset, and emotional responses. Now, let's explore a common challenge in personal growth that might arise—resistance to change. We'll delve into why individuals often resist changing their behavior, even when they are aware of the potential benefits.

BREAKING THROUGH RESISTANCE TO CHANGE

While we recognize the benefits of change and may even desire it, we often find ourselves stuck in old patterns. So, why do we resist changing our behavior, even when it could improve our lives? Here are some common reasons:

- **Fear of the Unknown:** Change brings uncertainty. We may worry about the consequences of stepping outside our comfort zone, or doubt our ability to adapt to new situations. It's natural to feel hesitant when facing the unknown.
- **Comfort in the Familiar:** The predictable, even if unsatisfying, can feel safer than the unknown. Old habits, even those that no longer serve us, provide a sense of familiarity and control.
- **Loss of Control:** Change can make us feel like we have less say in our lives. This perceived loss of control can be unsettling, especially if we're used to being in charge.
- **Emotional Investment:** Sometimes, we've invested so much time, energy, or emotional resources into the current way of things that letting go feels daunting. It's easy to feel a sense of attachment to our past choices, even if a change would ultimately be beneficial.

Tips for Overcoming Change Resistance

Thankfully, resistance doesn't have to be a permanent roadblock. Here are ways to confront it and embrace change for personal growth:

- **Start Small:** Instead of radical overnight shifts, break down your change goals into manageable steps. This reduces the overwhelm and builds a sense of accomplishment as you progress. For instance, if you want to be more assertive, start by practicing speaking up in a low-stakes situation before gradually working your way up to more challenging scenarios.
- **Adopt a Growth Mindset:** View challenges as opportunities to learn and grow, rather than insurmountable obstacles. Remember, setbacks are temporary and a normal part of the learning process. Reframe these moments as chances to adapt and refine your approach.
- **Focus on the Benefits:** Keep a detailed list of the positive reasons behind your desire to change. Visualize the improved life that change can bring. Refer back to this list when resistance feels strong, reminding yourself of the bigger picture.
- **Celebrate Wins:** Acknowledge and reward even small victories along the way. This positive reinforcement will fuel your motivation and keep you going. Did you speak up for yourself in a meeting today? Treat yourself to your favorite coffee or spend extra time on a cherished hobby.
- **Seek Support:** Don't go it alone. Share your goals with trusted friends, family members, or mentors. Their encouragement and perspective can be invaluable. If you

need additional support, a coach or therapist can provide personalized guidance and accountability to help you stay on track.

Strategies for Embracing Change

Here are some additional techniques to help you move through resistance and successfully navigate change:

- **Write It Down:** Putting your goals and fears on paper brings them into focus. Journaling can be a powerful way to process your feelings, identify potential obstacles, and create action plans to overcome them.
- **Accept Your Fears:** It's natural to feel anxiety or self-doubt during change. Instead of fighting these feelings, acknowledge them as part of the process. Remind yourself of your reasons for embracing change, and take small steps forward despite your fear.
- **Embrace Creative Thinking:** Change often requires fresh perspectives and innovative solutions. Brainstorm multiple approaches to a problem, experiment with new ideas, and don't be afraid to step outside of your comfort zone.
- **Build Community:** Surround yourself with people who support your growth. Share your goals with trusted friends, family, or consider joining a group of like-minded individuals. Having a support network provides encouragement, accountability, and the knowledge that you're not alone.

Mindfulness and self-care, concepts we've often touched on throughout the book, are also essential tools for overcoming resistance. Mindfulness techniques help you stay present and manage anxiety during change, while prioritizing healthy habits supports your overall well-being and strengthens your resilience.

But sometimes, the most significant barrier to embracing change and unlocking your full potential comes from within. A common culprit is imposter syndrome.

ADDRESSING IMPOSTOR SYNDROME

Despite achieving remarkable success, you may still struggle with a nagging feeling that you're not truly deserving, that it's all a fluke. This disconnect between external accomplishments and your internal experience is known as imposter syndrome. It can sabotage your potential and hold you back from fully embracing growth and change.

Why does this disconnect happen? Imposter syndrome can stem from a variety of factors, including:

- **Family Environment:** Growing up with highly critical parents or in a family that placed excessive emphasis on achievement can make it difficult to internalize success. It conditions you to always look for external validation and leaves you with a deep-rooted fear of not being good enough.
- **Social Pressures:** Constantly comparing yourself to others, especially in an era where social media presents curated, perfect images, can fuel self-doubt and make you feel like you don't measure up.
- **Sense of Belonging:** If you feel like an outsider in a particular field or workplace, perhaps due to race, gender, background, or other factors, it can make you question

your legitimacy and competence, even when you possess the necessary skills.

- **New Challenges or Roles:** Taking on a new job, project, or leadership role can trigger imposter feelings, especially if it involves a significant leap outside your comfort zone. The unfamiliar territory can lead you to doubt your abilities and amplify self-critical voices.
- **Past Negative Feedback:** If you've had particularly harsh or unfair criticism in the past, it can linger in your mind and fuel feelings of inadequacy, even if your current performance is exceptional.

Certain personality traits make some individuals more susceptible. Perfectionism can lead to constantly setting impossibly high standards, making it difficult to celebrate success. Anxiety or a tendency toward self-criticism can amplify negative thoughts, fueling the imposter cycle. These traits also influence how imposter syndrome manifests itself in your own life. Some common ways it can show up include:

- **Self-doubt: A constant questioning of your abilities and worthiness.** This deep-seated self-doubt can make you dismiss positive feedback, feel like a phony, and constantly worry that you'll disappoint others despite any past achievements.
- **Undervaluing Contributions: Downplaying your own role in achievements.** You might find it difficult to accept credit for your successes, minimizing your skills and talents while emphasizing the contributions of others.
- **Attributing Success to External Factors: Believing luck or timing, rather than skill, led to your success.** Instead of recognizing your hard work and abilities, you might attribute accomplishments to being "in the right place at

the right time," rather than acknowledging your own merit.

- **Sabotaging Self-Success: Procrastination, over-preparation, or avoiding challenges for fear of being "found out."** Fear of failure and exposure as a fraud can lead to either under-preparing (procrastinating) or overcompensating (over-preparing) to an unhealthy degree. You might avoid taking risks or challenges that could expose your perceived limitations.
- **Setting Unrealistic Expectations: Holding yourself to impossible standards.** Perfectionism often fuels this trait, leaving you constantly dissatisfied with your work. Even when achieving great things, you may focus on the smallest imperfection, preventing you from enjoying your accomplishments.
- **Continuous Fear: The unending worry of not living up to expectations and being exposed as a fraud.** This persistent anxiety can be exhausting, undermining your self-confidence and making it difficult to focus on the present moment due to a constant fear of being "found out."
- **Burnout: Pushing yourself relentlessly out of a need to "prove" yourself.** The relentless drive to overcompensate and maintain the façade of competence can lead to burnout. This can manifest as physical and emotional exhaustion, cynicism, and decreased effectiveness.
- **Difficulty Accepting Compliments: Struggling to internalize positive feedback.** You might deflect, dismiss, or feel uncomfortable with compliments since they contradict your internal belief about your worthiness.
- **Overly Sensitive to Criticism: Experiencing even constructive feedback as devastating.** It reinforces your fear of being a fraud and makes you question your abilities.

- **Comparison to Others: Habitually comparing yourself to colleagues or peers, always finding yourself lacking.** This leads to a constant sense of inadequacy and fuels self-doubt.
- **Fear of Speaking Up: Avoiding sharing your ideas or asking questions.** You fear exposing your perceived incompetence or lack of knowledge.

It's easy to see how these characteristics of imposter syndrome can create a vicious cycle of self-doubt and sabotage, with devastating consequences for your personal and professional growth. The good news is, imposter syndrome doesn't need to define you. There are effective strategies to challenge your inner critic and regain a sense of confidence in your abilities.

- **Understand the Voice:** Notice the patterns of your inner critic. Is it judgmental? Harsh? Does it use words like "always" or "never"? Recognizing these patterns helps you separate the critical voice from your true identity.
- **Assess the Evidence:** Write down a list of your achievements, strengths, and positive feedback you've received. Refer back to this list when imposter feelings arise, actively countering negative thoughts with objective reality.
- **Refocus on Values:** Connect your goals and actions to your core values—what matters most to you? Centering yourself on your values gives your work deeper meaning and lessens the need for external validation.
- **Reframe Around Growth:** Approach challenges and setbacks as opportunities for learning and development. Remind yourself that mistakes are a normal part of the growth process, not proof of incompetence.

- **Get Out of Your Head:** Talk to a trusted mentor, therapist, or friend about your imposter feelings. Sharing your fears can bring a fresh perspective and help you see yourself more realistically.
- **Practice Self-Compassion:** Cultivate a kinder inner voice. When you catch yourself engaging in negative self-talk, ask yourself: "Would I speak to a friend this way?" Offer yourself the same understanding and forgiveness you would to others.
- **Keep Failure in Perspective:** Remember that everyone fails sometimes. Focus on what you can learn from the experience and how you can adapt for the future, instead of dwelling on past setbacks.
- **Be Mindful:** Mindfulness practices help you develop the ability to observe your thoughts and emotions without getting caught up in them. This allows you to recognize imposter thoughts as they arise and prevent them from spiraling out of control.
- **Seek Trusted Feedback:** Regularly ask mentors, colleagues, or even trusted friends for honest assessments of your strengths and areas for improvement. This helps you gain a more balanced view of your abilities and potential.

Developing your EI provides powerful tools for overcoming imposter syndrome. Let's explore how each of the five pillars of EI can support you:

- **Self-Awareness:** EI helps you identify and understand the patterns of your inner critic. Recognizing these thoughts as distortions, rather than reality, is the first step toward combating them.

- **Self-Regulation:** EI empowers you to manage negative thoughts and emotions, preventing them from spiraling out of control. You learn to challenge your inner critic and reframe situations without getting overwhelmed.
- **Motivation:** Understanding your values and what drives you can help you push past negative thinking. Your motivation allows you to acknowledge your accomplishments and virtues as drivers towards your goals.
- **Empathy:** Practicing empathy towards yourself fosters self-compassion. By understanding and being kind to yourself, as you would be to a friend, you can break the cycle of harsh, imposter-driven criticism.
- **Social Skills:** Enhanced social skills allow you to build supportive relationships and tap into the power of mentorship. Sharing your experiences with trusted individuals helps you feel less alone and gain valuable perspectives that challenge your self-limiting beliefs.

Developing your EI and applying the strategies we've discussed will empower you to build a growth mindset, while keeping imposter syndrome at bay. However, maintaining motivation and resilience when progress feels slow or challenges arise is another key aspect of achieving your goals. There are strategies to promote commitment and perseverance, even when the going gets tough.

MAINTAINING MOTIVATION AMIDST CHALLENGES

The path of personal growth is rarely a straight line. There will be times when progress feels frustratingly slow or obstacles seem insurmountable. Maintaining your motivation during these challenging periods is essential for achieving your goals. Here are key strategies to keep your spirits high and stay committed:

- **Focus on the "Why":** Reconnect with the personal reasons behind your goals when enthusiasm dwindles. Visualize the benefits of achieving them to reignite your passion.
- **Set Realistic Goals:** Break down large goals into smaller, achievable milestones. This keeps you motivated as you see tangible progress, making the overall goal feel less daunting.
- **Find Inspiration:** Read stories, watch videos, or listen to podcasts featuring individuals who've overcome adversity and achieved their goals. Their journeys can be a powerful source of motivation.
- **Recognize Your Roadblocks:** Be honest about what's holding you back. Is it lack of time, fear of failure, or limiting beliefs? Identifying these roadblocks allows you to develop strategies for overcoming them.
- **Be Nice to Yourself:** Practice self-compassion, especially during setbacks. Remember, everyone experiences challenges. Treat yourself with the same kindness and understanding you would offer a friend who is struggling.
- **Celebrate Victories:** Acknowledge and celebrate both small and significant wins along the way. This reinforces positive behaviors and generates the momentum to keep going.
- **Reward Yourself:** Create a system of rewards for reaching milestones. This could be anything from a relaxing bath to a new book.
- **Have a Support System:** Surround yourself with people who believe in you and your potential. Mentors, friends, or family members can offer encouragement, advice, and a sense of accountability when your resolve wavers.

Throughout this chapter, we've explored strategies to address common roadblocks along your EI journey—from overcoming skepticism and resistance to change to battling imposter syndrome. Challenges are natural parts of the growth process. With each obstacle you face, you become stronger, wiser, and more emotionally intelligent. Let's continue this journey by exploring ways to integrate and sustain EI growth for lasting change.

CHAPTER EIGHT

SUSTAINING EI GROWTH

I t's a typical Monday morning. You wake with a start, glancing at your phone. Your heart starts to race as you realize you forgot to set an alarm. You're late for work. The notifications are rolling in, and you can see that your inbox, already overwhelming, is spilling over. Is that a flicker of anger at yourself, or a surge of anxiety for falling behind on a busy day? The simple act of identifying the emotion offers the first step towards control (Lieberman et al., 2007), a testament to the power of self-awareness you've already begun to cultivate.

Later, a tense meeting calls for careful navigation. Instead of impulsive reactions, you consciously employ active listening strategies. Your words and approach to the situation are calm and measured. Progress is made where there may have otherwise been conflict, highlighting the positive impact of the emotional regulation skills you've honed.

A mid-afternoon coffee with an old friend turns into a heart-to-heart. They confide in you, their frustration clear. Resisting the urge to immediately offer solutions, you instead focus on the empathy skills you've practiced. You provide a listening ear and a safe space—true support grounded in a deep understanding of their emotional landscape. You leave feeling like you've built an even closer connection, and deepened your already meaningful relationship (Davis, 1983).

The day finally ends. Instead of spiraling into stress-fueled over-whelm, you utilize relaxation techniques, actively choosing a calmer path. The physiological benefits are tangible as you feel the stress dissipating from your body. Relaxed, you quickly fall into a restful sleep, preparing you for the day ahead.

Now imagine these same scenarios without the EI tools you've begun to master. The heightened stress, the potential for misunderstandings, the missed opportunities for connec-tion—this highlights the real-world difference EI makes in your life. The most exciting part is that you have the capacity to continuously expand these skills. Our brains have an incredible capacity for adaptability. This, coupled with a growth mindset—the belief in our potential to change—unlocks limitless possibilities within your EI journey (Dweck, 2007).

True transformation comes from making EI an ingrained practice that shapes how you experience life—your challenges, your rela-tionships, even your understanding of yourself. As you embrace continuous growth, prioritize self-care, and cultivate support, the rewards of living with EI await you.

A GROWTH MINDSET

Do you believe your EI abilities can be developed, or are they set in stone? The answer lies in understanding the difference between a growth mindset and a fixed mindset.

Individuals with a growth mindset hold a powerful belief: their skills, including EI, can be cultivated and improved with effort and time. They see challenges as stepping stones, embrace learning, and persevere in the face of setbacks. In contrast, those with a fixed mindset view their abilities as innate and unchangeable. They may avoid challenges, fearing they expose a lack of talent, and become discouraged by obstacles.

Your mindset shapes how you approach the very process of developing your emotional intelligence. With a fixed mindset, facing an emotional challenge or recognizing a deficit in your EI skills can fuel a sense of inadequacy. This often leads to disengagement, as you may believe that no amount of effort will change the outcome.

A growth mindset transforms this experience. Challenges become opportunities. Setbacks offer valuable insights for future strategies. Recognizing areas for development becomes motivation for growth. This mindset empowers you to persist through the inevitable ups and downs of your EI journey, knowing that each experience strengthens your skills and expands your capabilities.

Tips to Develop a Growth Mindset

Cultivating a growth mindset is a transformative process. Here are some practical strategies to help you along the way:

- **Practice Self-Reflection:** Take time to honestly examine your beliefs about your intelligence and abilities. Do you find yourself saying, "I'm just not good with people," or "I can't control my temper"? Challenge these statements by looking for past examples of when you successfully navigated a complex situation or managed a difficult emotion. Recognizing even small victories can shift your thinking towards growth.

- **Visualize Success:** Before facing a challenging situation, visualize yourself handling it with calmness, confidence, and strong EI skills.
- **Give Yourself a Pep Talk:** The internal dialogue you have with yourself significantly impacts your mindset. Instead of self-criticism, reframe challenges with positive language. Instead of thinking "I'm screwing this up," try, "This is difficult, but I'm learning and can improve over time."
- **Embrace Challenges:** Seek out opportunities that stretch your current EI abilities. Join a public speaking group if social situations make you anxious, or intentionally navigate a difficult conversation with a colleague instead of avoiding it.
- **View Failure as a Learning Opportunity:** When things don't go as planned, don't let it derail your progress. Instead of dwelling in discouragement, analyze what happened. What could you have done differently? What did you learn that you can use the next time you face a similar situation?
- **Mind Your Language:** Pay attention to the words you use. Replace "I can't" with "I can't *yet*," or "I'm working on it." Subtle shifts in your language reinforce a belief in your potential to grow and change.
- **Seek Feedback, Not Just Approval:** While it's great to feel validated, ask for specific feedback to identify areas for growth.
- **Foster a Love for Learning:** Read books, attend workshops, or find online resources that delve into the areas of EI you want to develop. Celebrate your progress along the way—recognizing those small wins fuels your motivation for continuous growth.

By actively nurturing a growth mindset, you set the stage for continuous development of your emotional intelligence. Challenges become catalysts for expansion, and setbacks offer valuable lessons for the future. To sustain this growth mindset, it's vital to prioritize self-care as a non-negotiable part of the EI journey. Developing emotional intelligence takes effort and mental energy, and self-care provides the respite and replenishment needed to sustain your growth over the long term.

THE ROLE OF SELF-CARE IN EI DEVELOPMENT

Your physical health, mental state, and emotional well-being are inextricably linked. Research demonstrates that factors like poor sleep, chronic stress, and unresolved emotional issues can significantly impact cognitive function, decision-making, and our ability to manage our own emotions (Extremera & Fernández-Berrocal, 2006).

With this interconnection in mind, it's clear that self-care plays a vital role in developing your emotional intelligence. When your physical and mental resources are depleted, it becomes incredibly challenging to be self-aware, regulate your emotions, practice empathy, or navigate social situations with skill. Self-care directly fuels the mental and emotional resources you need to cultivate your emotional intelligence.

The Value of Self-Care

Self-care is often framed as a way to manage stress or indulge in moments of relaxation. While these are important benefits, true self-care goes much deeper. At its core, it's about fostering a healthy relationship with yourself by recognizing and meeting your own needs on all levels—physical, mental, emotional, and beyond.

Some might think self-care is just about doing what feels good in the moment—that it's inherently "selfish." This misconception couldn't be further from the truth. When you prioritize your own well-being, you're actually better equipped to be present for others. You have the energy and focus to be a good friend, supportive partner, or effective team member. Self-care isn't about withdrawing from the world but rather engaging with it from a place of inner strength and stability.

Common Self-Care Myths

Several pervasive myths prevent people from fully embracing self-care practices. Let's dispel some of the most common ones:

- **Myth 1: Self-care is all or nothing.** The truth is, even small acts of self-care can be incredibly powerful. A five-minute meditation, a nourishing meal, or a short walk in nature can significantly benefit your well-being. Don't fall into the trap of thinking it has to be time-consuming or elaborate to matter.
- **Myth 2: Self-care isn't for everyone.** This simply isn't true. Regardless of your circumstances or personality, self-care practices can be tailored to fit your life. It's about identifying what replenishes you, both in the moment and over time.
- **Myth 3: Self-care requires resources you don't have.** While some self-care activities might involve a cost (like a gym membership or a art class), many effective practices are completely free. Think about utilizing nature, engaging

in mindfulness exercises, or simply setting boundaries to protect your time and energy.

- **Myth 4: Self-care is anything that feels good in the moment.** While a bubble bath or binge-watching your favorite show can be relaxing, self-care also goes much deeper. It's about addressing underlying needs, not just providing a temporary escape.
- **Myth 5: Self-care is selfish.** As we've discussed, this myth misrepresents the true nature of self-care. By taking care of yourself, you actually enhance your capacity to care for and connect with others in a meaningful way. Investing in your well-being has a positive ripple effect, not a negative one.

Self-care looks different for everyone. The key is finding what works best for you across various dimensions of wellness. Remember, the most effective approach is one that fits your individual needs and preferences. With this in mind, let's explore some self-care practices specifically geared towards strengthening your emotional intelligence:

- **Physical:** Prioritizing sleep, nourishing your body with healthy foods, and engaging in regular exercise directly impact your stress levels, energy, and overall focus—all essential components for effectively managing your emotions.
- **Mental:** Embracing a love of learning through reading, puzzles, or creative activities sharpens your mind. This enhances your cognitive function, supporting clear thinking and sound decision-making, even during emotionally challenging moments.
- **Emotional:** Journaling, seeking out a therapist or trusted confidant, and practicing stress-reduction techniques are

all ways to nurture your emotional well-being. This builds self-awareness and gives you the tools to navigate difficult emotions skillfully.

- **Environmental:** Creating a calming and organized living space, along with immersing yourself in nature, reduces anxiety and enhances focus. This creates a greater capacity for staying present and engaged during your interactions with others.
- **Financial:** Developing a budget and working towards financial stability reduces a significant source of stress that can undermine your mental bandwidth. Taking control of your finances fosters a sense of security that supports your overall well-being, including your EI.
- **Social:** Spending quality time with supportive loved ones or joining like-minded communities boosts your mood and creates a sense of belonging. Feeling connected makes it easier to reach out for support and navigate complex social situations.
- **Recreational:** Engaging in hobbies, listening to music, and simply allowing yourself time for pure enjoyment lowers stress and provides the space for emotional rejuvenation.
- **Spiritual:** Practicing meditation, engaging in contemplation, or connecting with your spiritual beliefs nurtures both self-awareness and a sense of greater meaning. This inner strength empowers you to face life's challenges with resilience, a hallmark of strong EI.

By consistently prioritizing your well-being across various aspects of your life, you create a solid foundation for ongoing EI growth. But your journey doesn't happen in a vacuum. The environment you surround yourself with also plays a significant role in your EI development.

CREATING A SUPPORTIVE ENVIRONMENT FOR EI GROWTH

Just as a plant needs fertile soil and sunlight to thrive, EI flourishes fully within a supportive environment. Surrounding yourself with people who believe in your potential, encourage honest self-reflection, and celebrate your growth acts as a powerful catalyst for your EI journey.

This is why building a supportive community matters:

- **Encouragement and belief:** People who genuinely see your strengths bolster your own belief in yourself, especially when facing challenges or setbacks. Their confidence in you helps cultivate the inner determination needed for continuous growth.
- **Positive Influence:** Our surroundings and social circles profoundly impact our behavior and outlook. Being in the company of people who value emotional intelligence, practice empathy, and communicate effectively helps normalize these behaviors, making them easier to adopt yourself.
- **Accountability:** A supportive network offers gentle accountability when needed. They can lovingly point out blind spots or challenge you to try a new approach, propelling your development.
- **Shared Journey:** Connecting with others pursuing EI growth fosters a sense of camaraderie. You can share tips, resources, and offer non-judgmental support through challenges, lessening the feeling of isolation and making the process more enjoyable.

When it comes to your supportive community, it's not about vastly expanding your social circle. Seek quality over quantity. There are some practical ways to build your community of EI-supportive individuals:

- **Seek Out Existing Relationships:** Do you already have friends, family, or colleagues who are naturally empathetic, demonstrate strong communication skills, and encourage your growth? Spend more intentional time with them, and let them know that you value their EI strengths.
- **Join Communities:** Consider taking a workshop, joining a class, or becoming a member of an online or in-person group focused on personal development. These environments attract like-minded individuals.
- **Volunteer:** Giving back not only benefits others but often puts you in contact with compassionate, self-aware individuals who could become positive influences.
- **Explore Hobbies and Interests:** Joining clubs or groups based on hobbies (like sports, book clubs, or creative pursuits) lets you connect with people over a shared interest, often leading to more meaningful interactions where EI naturally comes into play.
- **Invest in Professional Connections:** Actively engage in professional organizations or networking groups within your field. Look for individuals who possess strong EI and seek opportunities to collaborate or learn from them.

Although supportive connections, both within your existing networks and through new communities, are important for your EI growth, sometimes, you need more specialized guidance. This is where having a mentor can be invaluable.

The Value of Mentorship for EI Growth

Mentors play a unique role in supporting your EI journey. A good mentor combines subject matter expertise with a genuine investment in your development. Specifically for EI growth, they provide valuable benefits:

- **Personalized Feedback:** Mentors offer honest, constructive feedback in a safe environment. They help you recognize patterns in your emotional responses and interpersonal interactions that may be difficult to see on your own.
- **Skill Development:** Mentors guide you in practicing specific EI skills. They might role-play challenging conversations, help you develop emotional regulation strategies, or suggest communication techniques, offering a space to try things out before facing real-life scenarios.
- **Accountability and Encouragement:** A good mentor balances support with challenging you to step outside your comfort zone. They recognize your potential and push you to reach for the next level of your EI development.

Choosing the right mentor is vital, as not everyone is equally equipped to support your specific EI development journey. Here are some essential characteristics to look for:

- **Strong EI:** A mentor should not just talk the talk but walk the walk. Look for individuals who consistently demonstrate the EI skills and behaviors you aspire to embody yourself.
- **Good Listener:** Mentorship relies on open and honest communication. Your mentor needs to be someone who

listens actively—not just hearing your words, but truly grasping your meaning and perspective.

- **Trust and Rapport:** For mentorship to be truly effective, you must feel safe and comfortable opening up about challenges, triumphs, and perhaps even things you might not share with others. Choose someone you feel a genuine connection with and potential for building trust.

- **Accessibility and Investment:** Ideally, a mentor should be available for regular interaction to provide consistent support. Look for someone who shows genuine interest in your growth and is willing to devote time and energy to helping you succeed.

- **Ability to Provide Constructive Feedback:** A good EI mentor offers both praise and thoughtful, honest feedback. They should help you identify areas for improvement without judgment and in a way that inspires you to grow.

- **A Growth Mindset:** Seek out mentors who embody a growth mindset, believing in the potential of both themselves and others. This mindset is contagious, fueling your own belief in your capacity to progress.

Mentorship doesn't always have to be a formal, one-on-one relationship. Consider these additional options:

- **Peer Mentorship:** Sometimes, mentors who are at a similar stage in their journey as you can be incredibly beneficial. Peer mentorship offers a unique sense of camaraderie, where you learn and grow together. It also provides an opportunity to practice active listening and support, which strengthens your own EI.

- **Online Mentorship:** Don't limit your mentor search by geography. Online platforms and communities often connect mentees with mentors from diverse locations and backgrounds. This expands your options, potentially allowing you to find someone with niche expertise in the EI areas you most want to develop.

- **Group Mentorship:** Some programs offer the opportunity for several individuals to learn from a single mentor. This model provides diverse perspectives and a built-in peer support system.

Biographies and autobiographies of historical or contemporary figures with strong EI can be incredibly valuable mentors. Their stories offer insights into effective decision-making, emotional management under pressure, and powerful communication. Selecting the right biographies makes all the difference. Consider these factors when finding your "literary mentors":

- **Relevance:** Are there specific EI skills you want to develop (for example, conflict resolution, empathy, or influencing others)? Seek out biographies of individuals known for excelling in those areas.
- **Time Period and Context:** Biographies set in different historical periods can offer valuable lessons in how EI was expressed within unique social and cultural contexts, broadening your understanding of interpersonal dynamics.
- **Diverse Voices:** Don't limit yourself to figures who resemble you. Reading about people from vastly different backgrounds, cultures, or professions can challenge your own assumptions and offer fresh perspectives on human behavior.
- **Author and Reviews:** Look for well-respected authors known for accurate and insightful portrayals of their subjects. Reviews offer clues about the writing style and

whether the biography focuses on areas relevant to your interests.

Look for figures in fields relevant to your own interests, as well as those with vastly different backgrounds to expand your perspective.

YOUR EI ENVIRONMENT TAKES MANY FORMS

Your supportive environment extends beyond people. Carefully consider the spaces you inhabit, both physical and virtual.

- **Home Environment:** Is your home a place of calm and relaxation, or a constant source of stress? De-cluttering, using soothing colors, and incorporating elements of nature can enhance your overall well-being, which supports EI during interactions with others.
- **Online Spaces:** Be mindful of the social media you consume. Are you following accounts that uplift and inspire, or those fueling negativity and comparison? Curate a virtual environment that fosters a positive mindset.
- **Community and Workplace:** Surround yourself with people who demonstrate the EI traits you wish to develop. Observe their actions, ask questions, and let them model healthier responses. Seek workplaces that prioritize emotional well-being, as such environments promote collaboration and make practicing your own skills easier.

It's important to recognize that creating a supportive environment is an ongoing process. As you evolve and your EI needs change, your network and surroundings may need adjusting as well. Regularly reassess the impact of your environment, making adjustments that amplify your growth. Intentionally shaping your surroundings creates a powerful feedback loop: a calmer home reduces your baseline stress, making it easier to be patient in difficult interactions; inspiring online content fuels your empathy and optimism; and supportive friends model the EI skills you want to embody. These positive influences, in turn, further strengthen your EI, leading to ever-greater success in all areas of your life.

CONCLUSION

Throughout your life, your emotions may have felt like a force you couldn't predict or control. Maybe they've steered you into impulsive decisions, sparked regrettable outbursts, or left you paralyzed by fear. Armed with the knowledge and tools contained in these pages, you can become the architect of your own inner world. Emotions will shift from being sources of chaos to valuable signals as you practice deciphering the messages they hold, harnessing their energy for positive action. This newfound understanding fosters a deep sense of self-mastery, and a life where your emotions serve you, rather than control you.

Consider how celebrities like Dwayne "The Rock" Johnson and Serena Williams embody these principles. The Rock's genuine charisma and ability to connect with audiences on a deep level stem from his strong EI. His self-awareness allows him to embrace both his vulnerabilities and his strengths, creating a persona that's both powerful and approachable. Serena Williams' dominance on the tennis court is undeniable, but her mental fortitude sets her apart. She understands the power of her emotions, using them to fuel her competitive spirit and maintain laser focus under intense pressure.

Think of the transformation this offers—in your workplace, relationships, and within yourself. From navigating difficult conversations with calm clarity to turning stress into fuel for growth, EI grants you the power to shape your experiences. No longer bound by old emotional patterns, you can embrace the possibilities that come from understanding and managing your inner world. Imagine becoming someone known for their resilience in the face of challenges, their authenticity, and their ability to deeply connect with others. This is the potential that EI unlocks.

But what does this transformation truly look like? These "before-and-after" examples paint a vivid picture of how EI can transform everyday life:

Workplace Success:

- Before: You're talented but overlooked for promotions, feeling frustrated that your technical skills aren't enough. Days drag by as you watch less capable colleagues climb the ladder.
- After: Your improved communication and ability to build strong team relationships make you a natural leader. You inspire others with your vision and earn respect by helping those around you shine. Success isn't just about what you do, but who you are.

Relationship Harmony

- Before: Arguments with your partner escalate quickly, leaving you both hurt and disconnected, caught in a cycle

of defensiveness. Resentment simmers beneath the surface, threatening the warmth you once shared.
- After: With deeper empathy and vulnerability, you navigate conflict together. Difficult conversations become opportunities to understand each other better, strengthening your bond with each hurdle you overcome.

Conquering Stress:

- Before: Anxiety gnaws at you constantly, making it hard to focus and robbing you of joy. You fear difficult situations will cause you to unravel, leaving you paralyzed by self-doubt.
- After: You've learned to calm your racing mind and reframe negative thoughts. Stressful events become challenges to overcome, not threats to your well-being. You approach obstacles with a newfound sense of inner peace and confidence.

Unleashing Personal Power

- Before: Your inner critic runs the show, doubting your worth and making you risk-averse. You play it small to avoid feeling like a failure, leaving your true potential untapped.
- After: You recognize those negative voices for what they are—old patterns, not truths. With self-compassion, you silence the critic and boldly pursue goals that align with your deepest values. You embrace the discomfort of growth, knowing that each step forward reveals a stronger, more authentic version of yourself.

Think of the transformation this offers—in your workplace, relationships, and within yourself. From navigating difficult conversations with calm clarity, to turning stress into fuel for growth, EI grants you the power to shape your experiences. No longer bound by old emotional patterns, you embrace the possibilities that come from understanding and managing your inner world. Imagine becoming someone known for their resilience in the face of challenges, their authenticity, and their ability to deeply connect with others. This is the potential that EI unlocks. The RISE framework is your guide for turning those "after" scenarios into your reality.

- **Recognition (R):** The knowledge of emotional science, your own patterns, and the impact of EI has laid the groundwork for change.
- **Integration Strategies (IS):** The tools and techniques you've learned will empower you to transform your experiences—mastering your emotions, navigating challenges with ease, and cultivating rich, meaningful relationships both personally and professionally.
- **Empowerment (E):** You now understand the value of a supportive environment, how to overcome obstacles, and maintain your EI practice for sustained growth.

RISE is the bridge between knowledge and the kind of life EI makes possible. Understanding the theory (Recognition) was the essential first step, but action (Integration) is where true transformation takes hold. This is where you learn to turn difficult emotions into fuel for action, handle stressful situations with clarity rather than reactivity, and build deeper connections based on empathy and openness. Nurtured in a supportive environment (Empowerment), this practice ensures your growth continues—not just for today, but for a lifetime.

Will you wait for a life of ease and grace to find you? Or will you seize the power that lies within these pages, taking those first courageous steps towards the person you were meant to be?

The choice is yours. What will you create?

REFERENCES

American Psychological Association. (2023, November). *Stress in America 2023*. APA. http://www.apa.org/news/press/releases/stress/2023/collective-trauma-recovery

Bar-On, R. (1988). *The development of an operational concept of psychological well-being* [Doctoral dissertation], Rhodes University, South Africa.

Berger, B. G. (1994). Coping with stress: The effectiveness of exercise and other techniques. *Quest, 46(1)*, 100–119. https://www.researchgate.net/publication/234634083_Coping_With_Stress_The_Effectiveness_of_Exercise_and_Other_Techniques

Bradberry, T., & Greaves, J. (2009). *Emotional intelligence 2.0*. TalentSmart. http://dspace.vnbrims.org:13000/xmlui/bitstream/handle/123456789/4938/Emotional%20Intelligence%202.0.pdf?sequence=1&isAllowed=y

Chaput, J. P., Dutil, C., Featherstone, R., Ross, R., Giangregorio, L., Saunders, T. J., & Carrier, J. (2020). Sleep timing, sleep consistency, and health in adults: A systematic review. *Applied Physiology, Nutrition, and Metabolism, 45(10)*, S232–S247. https://pubmed.ncbi.nlm.nih.gov/33054339/

Cherniss, C. (2010). Emotional intelligence: Toward clarification of a concept. *Industrial and Organizational Psychology, 3(2)*, 110–126. https://www.researchgate.net/publication/229545635_Emotional_Intelligence_Toward_Clarification_of_a_Concept

Cherniss, C., Goleman, D., Emmerling, R., Cowan, K., & Adler, M. (1998). *Bringing emotional intelligence to the workplace*. New Brunswick, NJ: Consortium for Research on Emotional Intelligence in Organizations, Rutgers University, 1–34. https://www.researchgate.net/publication/316506268_Bringing_Emotional_Intelligence_to_the_Workplace_A_Technical_Report_Issued_by_the_Consortium_for_Research_on_Emotional_Intelligence_in_Organizations

Darwin, C. (1872). *The expression of the emotions in man and animals* (P. Ekman, Ed.). John Murray.

Davis, M. H. (1983). Measuring individual differences in empathy: Evidence for a multidimensional approach. *Journal of Personality and Social Psychology*, 44(1), 113–126. https://doi.org/10.1037/0022-3514.44.1.113

Duval, S., & Wicklund, R. A. (1973). Effects of objective self-awareness on attribution of causality. *Journal of Experimental Social Psychology, 9(1)*, 17–31. https://www.sciencedirect.com/science/article/abs/pii/0022103173900590

Dweck, C. S. (2007). *Mindset: The new psychology of success.* Random House Trade Paperbacks.

Ekman, P. (1999). Facial expressions. In T. Dalgleish, M. Power (Eds.), *Handbook of cognition and emotion,* 16(301). Wiley. https://onlinelibrary.wiley.com/doi/10.1002/0470013494.ch16

Emmerling, R. J., & Goleman, D. (2003). Emotional intelligence: Issues and common misunderstandings. *Issues and Recent Developments in Emotional Intelligence, 1(1),* 1–32. https://www.eiconsortium.org/reprints/ei_issues_and_common_misunderstandings.html

Extremera, N., & Fernández-Berrocal, P. (2006). Emotional intelligence as predictor of mental, social, and physical health in university students. *The Spanish Journal of Psychology, 9(1),* 45–51. https://pubmed.ncbi.nlm.nih.gov/16673622/

Gardner, H. (1975). *The shattered mind.* Knopf

Goddu, J. (2021, January 27). *The importance of emotional intelligence in leadership today.* Sogolytics Blog. http://www.sogolytics.com/blog/eq-the-importance-of-emotional-intelligence-in-leadership-today/

Goleman, D. (1995). *Emotional intelligence.* Bantam Books.

Goleman, Daniel. (2011, November 1). *They've taken emotional intelligence too far.* Time. https://ideas.time.com/2011/11/01/theyve-taken-emotional-intelligence-too-far/

Goudreau, J. (2013, October 10). *Jack Welch on how to manage millennial employees.* Business Insider. https://www.businessinsider.com/jack-welch-on-managing-millennial-employees-2013-10

Isaacson, W. (2012, April). *The real leadership lessons of Steve Jobs.* Harvard Business Review. http://hbr.org/2012/04/the-real-leadership-lessons-of-steve-jobs

Jacobson, E. (1938). *Progressive relaxation.* University of Chicago.

Jensen, E. (2005). *Teaching with the brain in mind.* ASCD.

Jobvite. (2020). *2020 Job seeker nation survey: When change is the only constant.* https://www.jobvite.com/wp-content/uploads/2020/05/FINAL-Jobvite-JobSeekerNation-Report1_5-11.pdf

Kaczmarek, B. L. (2020). Current views on neuroplasticity: What is new and what is old? *Acta Neuropsychologica, 18,* 1–14. https://www.researchgate.net/publication/340459197_CURRENT_VIEWS_ON_NEUROPLASTICITY_WHAT_IS_NEW_AND_WHAT_IS_OLD

Kaur, J., & Junnarkar, M. (2017). Emotional intelligence and intimacy in relationships. *The International Journal of Indian Psychology, 4(3),* 27–35. https://ijip.in/wp-content/uploads/ArticlesPDF/article_ee11515dd053f26a1e51c6bd5200eec7.pdf

Klein, G. (2004). *The power of intuition: How to use your gut feelings to make better decisions at work.* Crown Currency.

Lieberman, M. D., Eisenberger, N. I., Crockett, M. J., Tom, S. M., Pfeifer, J. H., & Way, B. M. (2007). Putting feelings into words: Affect labeling disrupts amygdala activity in response to affective stimuli. *Psychological Science, 18*(5), 421–428. https://pubmed.ncbi.nlm.nih.gov/17576282/

Luft, J., & Ingham, H. (1961). The Johari window. *Human Relations Training News, 5*(1), 6-7. https://static1.1.sqspcdn.com/static/f/1124858/28387950/1617395004320/THE+JOHARI+WINDOW.pdf

Maslow, A. H. (1950). Social theory of motivation. *Twentieth century mental hygiene: New directions in mental health,* 347-357. Social Sciences Publishers.

Mayer, J. D., & Salovey, P. (1993). The intelligence of emotional intelligence. *Intelligence, 17*(4), 433–442. https://www.sciencedirect.com/science/article/abs/pii/0160289693900103

Mayer, J. D., Salovey, P., Caruso, D. R., & Sitarenios, G. (2003). Measuring emotional intelligence with the MSCEIT V2.0. *Emotion,* 3(1), 97–105. https://pubmed.ncbi.nlm.nih.gov/12899321/

Miranda, D. (2023, April 27). *10 management styles of effective leaders.* Forbes Advisor. http://www.forbes.com/advisor/business/management-styles/#10_management_styles_of_effective_leaders_section.

Mischel, W. (2015). *The marshmallow test: Why self-control is the engine of success.* Little, Brown.

Payne, W. L. (1985). *A study of emotion: developing emotional intelligence; self-integration; relating to fear, pain and desire* [Dissertation], The Union for Experimenting Colleges and Universities. https://philpapers.org/rec/PAYASO

Ratiu, P., Talos, I. F., Haker, S., Lieberman, D., & Everett, P. (2004). The tale of Phineas Gage, digitally remastered. *Journal of Neurotrauma, 21*(5), 637–643. https://pubmed.ncbi.nlm.nih.gov/15165371/

Rogers, C. R. (1995). *On becoming a person: A therapist's view of psychotherapy.* Houghton Mifflin Harcourt.

Rooney, C., McKinley, M. C., & Woodside, J. V. (2013). The potential role of fruit and vegetables in aspects of psychological well-being: A review of the literature and future directions. *Proceedings of the Nutrition Society, 72*(4), 420–432. https://pubmed.ncbi.nlm.nih.gov/24020691/

Schwantes, M. (2023, November 3). *Richard Branson says the thing we all fear the most is actually the way to success.* Inc.com. https://www.inc.com/marcel-schwantes/richard-branson-says-thing-we-all-fear-most-is-actually-way-to-success.html

Sivanjali, M. (2021). Role of emotional intelligence in leadership and organizational success. *International Journal of Research and Innovation in Social Science, 5*(5), 315–

318. https://www.researchgate.net/publication/352658823_Role_of_Emotion al_Intelligence_in_Leadership_and_Organizational_success

The feelings wheel: Unlock the power of your emotions. (2023, August 29). Calm Blog. https://www.calm.com/blog/the-feelings-wheel

Thorndike, R. L., & Stein, S. (1937). An evaluation of the attempts to measure social intelligence. *Psychological Bulletin, 34*(5), 275. https://psycnet.apa.org/record/ 1937-03825-001

Tublin, P. A. (2014, December 13). *Microsoft's Nadella & unconscious bias toward women.* HuffPost. https://www.huffpost.com/entry/microsofts-nadella-uncon_b_5977214

Willcox, G. (1982). The feeling wheel: A tool for expanding awareness of emotions and increasing spontaneity and intimacy. *Transactional Analysis Journal, 12*(4), 274–276. https://journals.sagepub.com/doi/10.1177/036215378201200411

Wang, Y., Chen, J., & Yue, Z. (2017). Positive emotion facilitates cognitive flexibility: An fMRI study. *Frontiers in Psychology, 8,* 272735. https://www.ncbi.nlm.nih. gov/pmc/articles/PMC5671657/

Ward, M. (2017, February 1). *Why Pepsico CEO Indra Nooyi writes letters to her employees' parents.* CNBC. https://www.cnbc.com/2017/02/01/why-pepsico-ceo-indra-nooyi-writes-letters-to-her-employees-parents.html

Zaccaro, A., Piarulli, A., Laurino, M., Garbella, E., Menicucci, D., Neri, B., & Gemignani, A. (2018). How breath-control can change your life: A systematic review on psycho-physiological correlates of slow breathing. *Frontiers in Human Neuroscience, 12,* 409421. https://www.ncbi.nlm.nih.gov/pmc/arti cles/PMC6137615/

www.ingramcontent.com/pod-product-compliance
Lightning Source LLC
Chambersburg PA
CBHW070714130626
46553CB00005B/1981